Josef von Sternberg

by andrew sarris

the films of Josef von Sternberg

the museum of modern art, new york

distributed by doubleday & co., inc., garden city, n. y.

ACKNOWLEDGMENTS

The author wishes to acknowledge with thanks the kindness of Alex Gottlieb and George K. Arthur in providing background information on MACAO and THE SALVATION HUNTERS respectively. The Film Department and the author wish to thank the following organizations for the loan of films for the exhibition "The Films of Josef von Sternberg" held at The Museum of Modern Art, November 1–14, 1965, and November 23, 1965—January 1, 1966: Columbia Pictures Corporation, George Eastman House, Paramount Pictures Corporation, Pathe Contemporary Films, Inc., Twelvetrees, Inc., and United World Films. The author is indebted to Eileen Bowser and Myron Gladstone for toiling over the manuscript, and Adrienne Mancia and Joanne Godbout for their cooperation in making the Josef von Sternberg retrospectives at The Museum of Modern Art so successful. Ralph Blasi, James Card, William K. Everson, Bob Goldstein, Joseph Longo, Andrew C. McKay, George Pratt, Mark Shivas, Eugene B. Stavis, Herman G. Weinberg, and Eloise Wright generously contributed stills, film, and research materials while Stephen Gottlieb and Eugene Archer aided the author with their incisive insights into the art of Josef von Sternberg. Finally, the author wishes to thank Josef von Sternberg for bringing so much beauty to the screen.

Title page: Josef von Sternberg and Gary Cooper during the filming of MOROCCO (1930)

Although Josef von Sternberg's directorial career spans almost thirty years, he was a meaningful force in the cinema primarily between 1927 and 1935, an interval we might ironically designate as his Paramount Period. Until very recently, even his work of this period had not been seriously evaluated since the mid-thirties, when movies were supposed to crackle crisply to the proletarian point. Sternberg was then considered slow, decadent, and self-indulgent, while gloriously ambiguous Marlene Dietrich was judged too rich for the people's blood—it was a time for bread, not cake. Paradoxically, Sternberg and Dietrich today look deeper and more dazzling than ever, while most of the cinema of the bread lines looks excessively mannered.

Even today, however, the art of Josef von Sternberg is too often subordinated to the mystique of Marlene Dietrich, with whom the director was associated in seven of his more familiar movies. Unfortunately, the Svengali-Trilby publicity that enshrouded THE BLUE ANGEL, MOROCCO, DISHONORED, SHANGHAI EXPRESS, BLONDE VENUS, THE SCARLET EMPRESS, and THE DEVIL IS A WOMAN obscured the more meaningful merits not only of these particular works but of Sternberg's career as a whole. In fact, the director's filtered feminine mystique neither originated nor disappeared with Marlene Dietrich, but ecstatically embraced such other photogenic features as those of Georgia Hale, Evelyn Brent, Betty Compson, Olga Baclanova, Esther Ralston, Fay Wray, Sylvia Sidney, Frances Dee, Laraine Day, Gene Tierney, and Janet Leigh. It is also part of the record that he made films before THE BLUE ANGEL and after THE DEVIL IS A WOMAN. At all times, Sternberg's cinema of illusion and delusion has transcended the personality of even his most glittering star the better to reflect his own vision.

Josef von Sternberg was born in Vienna on May 29, 1894. His family emigrated to New York City when he was seven, and he attended public school there for three years, after which he and his parents returned to Vienna. They came back to the United States in 1908, and the following year Sternberg became a high school dropout to work first as a helper in a millinery shop, then in the stock room of a Fifth Avenue lace house. He recalls this period with grudging gratitude in his autobiography, *Fun in a Chinese Laundry*.

"My apprenticeship in the arts," he writes, "began in a millinery shop under the arch of a roaring elevated train, next to which I also slept at home. Tuition consisted in cleaning the shop, its windows, and the sidewalk, and a dark, grated cellar filled with a disarray of discarded ribbons, artificial cherries, manikins, and hat forms. This link to my past belonged to an aunt, whose son had managed to obtain an influential position in New York City, and before long I found myself employed in the stock room of a large lace house on Fifth Avenue. . . . After some weeks I became familiar with the differences between Venetian lace and rose point, Alençon, Chantilly, Valenciennes, Brussels, and Swiss. To be fair to my former employer, it occurs to me that this painfully acquired knowledge may have bobbed up in my films in my use of coarse fishnets to conceal some of the actors."

Sternberg moved in 1911 from fabric to film to serve as apprentice to a man who cleaned, patched and coated motion picture stock—often moonlighting as projectionist in a nearby movie theatre after work. His official film credits begin in 1914 at the World Film Corporation studios in Fort Lee, New Jersey, where he worked his way from film patcher and shipping clerk to chief assistant to William A. Brady, the head of the company. During the First World War, Sternberg produced some training films and was later stationed in Washington, D. C. as a Signal Corps photographer. He returned to his old job briefly after the war, then set out on his own as cutter, editor, writer, and assistant director. In these capacities, he worked in the Fort Lee studios, hopped to England for a short stay, and finally went West to Hollywood, still a relatively young man.

The story of Sternberg's early years contains gaps that have been filled from time to time with Hollywood back-fence gossip. Sternberg himself dismisses the widely circulated legend that he was once a Brooklyn pants-presser named Joe Stern. Nonetheless, the shuffling-to-and-fro circumstances of his life lent an aura of ambiguity to both his name and his nationality. It is not entirely clear, for example, whether his given name was Josef, Joe, or Jo. About the "von," however, there is now no mystery. It was coined for the credits of a 1924 film aptly enough entitled BY DIVINE RIGHT, in which he served as writer and assistant director.

"When the film was finished," Sternberg recalls in his autobiography, "the director, Roy William Neill, and the star, Elliot Dexter, who also financed the film, placed my name among the numerous credits that littered its beginning, and in order not to disturb the euphonic array of names that distinguished this undistinguished work, elongated my name. Jo Sternberg was stretched into an aristocratic Josef von Sternberg without my knowledge and without consulting me."

Sternberg does not duck responsibility for the accretion of the affectation. "Had I been consulted," he concedes, "I'm certain that I would have attached no importance to this implied baronetcy, for every kind of aristocrat was a dime a dozen, including princes and archdukes who walked the streets. It was in 1923, the recent war had crumbled one empire after the other, and members of the nobility had become doormen in Paris, cab drivers in New York, and extra players in Hollywood.

"But lo and behold, no sooner had the film been shown, than the press singled out this new 'aristocrat' for attack. It seemed that I had been chosen to represent the 'Huns' who recently had been defeated, and who were now about to invade Hollywood. The sacred territory of motion pictures was apparently in danger. All criticism of the content of the film centered around the 'von,' and somehow this absurd bombardment made me determine to continue using the silly addition, though it turned out to be a target for much longer than I expected."

Sternberg's first official credit as assistant director appears in connection with THE MYSTERY OF THE YELLOW ROOM. The year was 1919, the year of Griffith's BROKEN BLOSSOMS and TRUE HEART SUSIE, Chaplin's SUNNYSIDE and A DAY'S PLEASURE, Erich von Stroheim's THE DEVIL'S PASSKEY, Cecil B. De Mille's MALE AND FEMALE, and from abroad Robert Wiene's THE CABINET OF DR. CALIGARI, Ernst Lubitsch's MADAME DU BARRY, Victor Sjöström's KARIN INGMARSDOTTER, Mauritz Stiller's ARNE'S TREASURE, and Abel Gance's J'ACCUSE.

Emile Chautard, the French director Sternberg assisted in THE MYSTERY OF THE YELLOW ROOM, hardly ranked with these giants, but he was invaluable to Sternberg, who singles him out for praise in *Fun in a Chinese Laundry*. By contrast, Sternberg has nothing favorable to say about Lawrence Windom, Roy William Neill, Howard Thurston, and Wallace Worsley, the other directors with whom he worked in this era.

Later, Sternberg cast Chautard in MOROCCO and

SHANGHAI EXPRESS. "I don't know if I proved to be of service to him," Sternberg writes in his autobiography, "but there is little doubt in my mind of his service to me. While at work on a film called THE MYSTERY OF THE YELLOW ROOM he carefully instructed me in the rudiments of his craft, graphically explaining his methods to me (none of which I have ever forgotten), and what is more he permitted me to direct a few scenes for him. . . . As a small example of the care he took in transferring his knowledge to me, he would place a chair for the camera and point out to me that all four legs were now visible in the lens, explaining that if less than four legs were seen to support a chair on the screen it will attract undue attention and some idiot might wait for that chair to fall over. This detail, which could appear to some to be ridiculous, alerted me to inspect everything before the camera through the lens and soon paved the way for me to appraise the dimensional impact of everything in front of the lens, including the value of light and shadow."

In a sense, Sternberg entered the cinema through the camera rather than the cutting room and thus became a lyricist of light and shadow rather than a master of montage. As his anecdote about Chautard's chair would indicate, he concentrated on the spatial integrity of his images rather than on their metaphorical juxtaposition. Sternberg's cinema, for better or worse, represented a distinctively Germanic camera viewpoint—from Murnau and Lang—in contrast to Eisenstein's fashionably Marxist montage. Rationales for composition and camera movement were rare in the thirties. Nevertheless, Aeneas Mackenzie wrote both appreciatively and perceptively of Sternberg's style for *Life and Letters Today* (London, 1936) in an article entitled, "Leonardo of the Lenses."

"To understand what Sternberg is attempting to do," Mackenzie maintains, "one must first appreciate that he imposes the limitations of the visual upon himself: he refuses to obtain any effect whatsoever save by means of pictorial composition. That is the fundamental distinction between von Sternberg and all other directors. Stage acting he declines, cinema in its conventional aspect he despises as mere mechanics, and dialogue he employs primarily for its value as integrated sound. The screen is his medium—not the camera. His purpose is to reveal the emotional significance of a subject by a series of magnificent canvases."

Any such process in itself, of course, would be purely illustrative, and totally impractical because of its static nature. Nevertheless, a successful von Sternberg film is completely dynamic. The movement of a play on the stage (or of a stage play on the screen) is obtained by means of the literary principle of dramatic impulsion, the so-called *filmic motion* is induced by a regulation of the length and succession of its individual scenes, and the progression of the factory-made "movie" is procured by the introduction of entertaining irrelevancies; yet, all of these moments are denied to Sternberg by the very nature of what he is attempting to accomplish.

"In lieu of them he relies upon long and elaborate shots, each of which is developed internally—by camera movement and dramatic lighting—to a point where it detonates into shock, surprise, or startling beauty. And it is by means of this Ford-like internal combustion that a von Sternberg film progresses in audience interest: before the effect of one emotional percussion has subsided, the next is under way. Consequently, the story does not move his picture; it is his picture which moves the story."

Mackenzie's was a voice with few echoes, and complaints about Sternberg's slowness continued in a decade which had no time for the studied and the deliberate. Worse still for Sternberg's reputation was his relative lack of interest in realist social themes. His ideological indifference was interpreted as an affront to popular critical standards of the period.

Sternberg confesses candidly to a blind spot where sociological and political matters were concerned. "Not only was I in Berlin when Hitler became chancellor and his storm troops were in action without my seeing a single brown shirt or hearing a *Heil Hitler,*" he writes in his autobiography, "but I was also in Austria a week or so before he took it over and had no knowledge that this would take place. I was in Japan shortly before it began its conquest of Asia, and the only military preparation I perceived was in the shape of a pleasant Japanese officer who was my companion on a train ride through Korea and Manchuria. I was on the border of Spain when the civil war was raging, and all I saw was a peaceful landscape. I was in Mussolini's Rome and had an afternoon with him while Ethiopia was being taken and talked with him about films without being aware that anything else was on his mind. I've been in the middle of revolutions, and

unless a firecracker exploded at my feet I didn't know what was going on. I've been approached by men who offered me high posts once the country was taken over, and it was not until long after that I realized that they were Communists. I talked with Alexander Berkman and Emma Goldman before they were deported to Russia, and I didn't know they were anarchists. A man I sailed with in Tokyo Bay is now in prison for passing on to unfriendly governments information gleaned from American servicemen he befriended: and in my many contacts with him, all I knew was that he was a most charming companion.

"For one who has so closely observed everything else but that which might be particularly important, this is convincing evidence of a peculiar and specific block. I am not harnessed with the blinders of a horse that prevent it from perceiving what is to the right and left, and I am unable to account for this unawareness. Certainly it did me no good not to know what went on in minds other than my own."

Sternberg's apology for his solipsism seems unnecessary today, but in the thirties he was castigated for not mounting the barricades. In this polemical period, even Sternberg's "von" provided ammunition for a sharp-shooting anti-Hollywood sniper like John Grierson. "With SHANGHAI EXPRESS," Grierson growled, "Joe Sternberg has become the great Josef von Sternberg, having given up the struggle for good: a director so successful that even Adolf Zukor is pleased to hold his hand for a brief condescending moment."

What Sternberg lacked for Grierson was Stroheim's mania for martyrdom. Sternberg was generally professional enough to finish the films he started and accept full responsibility for them. He crossed the sound barrier and confronted the star system without sacrificing his style; and worst of all, he defended Hollywood at a time when it was intellectually unfashionable to do so. There is no reason to doubt that if the path to purer personal expression had been less contingent on financial considerations, Sternberg's career would have shown a higher ratio of art to craft. The artistic ratio is respectably high as it is, however, so that his work can be measured more by his actual achievements than by his alleged aspirations—that is, by his cinema rather than his metacinema.

Sternberg's image of himself remained that of the artist rather than the craftsman, the poet rather than the pro, and he knew better than anyone the nebulousness of the director's *métier*. "The so-called director, very often a most irritating person," he writes ruefully, "would have been eliminated long ago were he not essential in the construction of a film, probably the only craft where such a man whose work remains invisible is tolerated."

The fact remains that Sternberg's work—being more visual—was more visible than that of most of his colleagues. Even with a mechanically meaningless assignment like MACAO, his visual signature smiles through the veils and nets like the Cheshire Cat *à la* Chautard. That he chose to come to terms with an often uncongenial creative environment simply marks him as an artist who preferred lighting up a small shadow to cursing the darkness.

Even today, however, critics and audiences may be reluctant to endorse Sternberg's story sense. Apart from "classical" assignments like AN AMERICAN TRAGEDY and CRIME AND PUNISHMENT, his plots seem far-fetched, his backgrounds bizarre, and his character motivations obscure, at least by conventional standards of storytelling. As in a dream, he has wandered through studio sets representing Imperial Russia (THE LAST COMMAND, THE SCARLET EMPRESS), China (SHANGHAI EXPRESS, THE SHANGHAI GESTURE), North Africa (MOROCCO), Spain (THE DEVIL IS A WOMAN), Austria (THE CASE OF LENA SMITH, DISHONORED), France (THE EXQUISITE SINNER), and Germany (THE BLUE ANGEL). Even his American locales focus primarily on the dregs or fringes of society from the festive criminality of UNDERWORLD, THE DRAG NET and THUNDERBOLT to the bawdy, brawling backwaters and back streets of THE SALVATION HUNTERS, DOCKS OF NEW YORK, and BLONDE VENUS. Everyday life, as such, seldom appears in Sternberg's cinema. His characters generally make their first entrance at a moment in their lives when there is no tomorrow. Knowingly or unknowingly, they have reached the end or the bottom, but they will struggle a short time longer, about ninety minutes of screen time, to discover the truth about themselves and those they love. Although there is much violence and death in Sternberg's world, there is relatively little action. The various murders, duels, executions, suicides, and assaults serve merely as poetic punctuation for lives drifting to their destinations in reflective repose. Death in this context is less a conclusion than a termination. The paradox of violence without action is supplemented by the paradox of virtue without morality. There are no codes or systems in these dream worlds; the characters retain their civilized graces despite the most desperate struggles for psychic survival, and it is their poise under pressure, their style under stress, that grants them a measure of heroic stature and stoic calm.

Sternberg's films are poetic without being symbolic. We need not search for slumbering allegories of Man and God and Life, but rather for a continuous stream of emotional autobiography. Sternberg's exoticism is then less a pretense than a pretext for objectifying personal fantasies. His equivalent literary genre is not the novel, nor the short story, nor the theatrical spectacle, but the closet drama unplayable but for the meaningful grace of gesture and movement. There persists an erroneous impression that the art of a MOROCCO or a SHANGHAI EXPRESS consists of the magnifying of trivialities. Yet there is nothing trivial about the size of Sternberg's emotions, and nothing disproportionate in the means employed to express them, critics from John Grierson to Susan Sontag notwithstanding. Also there is conscious humor in the director's awareness of his own absurdity though some spectators still imagine they are laughing *at* Sternberg when they are actually laughing *with* him. The colorful costumes, the dazzling décors, the marble-pillared palaces merely underscore by ironic contrast the painfully acquired wisdom of the all too human prisoners of grandiose illusions. The limitations of this aesthetic are self-evident. An insufficient grasp of one's time and place is hardly a positive virtue even for the most lyrical poet. It is only when we look around at the allegedly significant cinema of Sternberg's contemporaries that we recognize the relative stature of a director who chose to write with a camera in the first person long before Alexandre Astruc's *"caméra-stylo"* made such impious subjectivity fashionable and such personal poetry comprehensible.

THE SALVATION HUNTERS (1925). George K. Arthur, Nellie Bly Baker, Georgia Hale, Otto Matiesen. The child, Bruce Guerin. Courtesy The National Film Archive, London

1925 THE SALVATION HUNTERS (Academy Pictures/United Artists) Directed and produced by Josef von Sternberg. Original script by Josef von Sternberg. Photographed by Edward Gheller. With George K. Arthur (The Boy), Georgia Hale (The Girl), Bruce Guerin (The Child), Otto Matiesen (The Man), Nellie Bly Baker (The Woman), Olaf Hytten (The Brute), and Stuart Holmes (The Gentleman).

THE SALVATION HUNTERS was born of a meeting between Sternberg and George K. Arthur; on this point both are agreed, although there are some discrepancies in their details. Curiously, Sternberg never identifies Arthur by name in *Fun in a Chinese Laundry,* but refers to the English actor-producer as "Kipps." Arthur, who had played the H. G. Wells character in a British movie, was at loose ends in Hollywood when he approached Sternberg to direct a comedy he had written entitled "Just Plain Bugs." Sternberg made a counter-proposal of his own script for THE SALVATION HUNTERS, and Arthur agreed to the substitution.

The financial details of the venture are both confused and controversial, but it seems probable that the final cost of the film was slightly under five thousand dollars and that at one crucial stage in the shooting Sternberg poured his savings into the budgetary breach. Arthur proved resourceful enough to have the finished film shown in the home of Charles Chaplin by bribing the star's butler. As a result, THE SALVATION HUNTERS was seen not only by Chaplin, but by Douglas Fairbanks, Mary Pickford, and Nicholas Schenck. Overnight Sternberg was recognized as a prodigy. Mary Pickford invited him to direct her next film, and Metro signed him for a long-term contract thereafter. Metro also signed Arthur to a seven-year acting contract, and the two were soon reunited in THE EXQUISITE SINNER.

Ultimately, *The New York Times* of Sunday, February 1, 1925, announced in its entertainment section: "THE SALVATION HUNTERS, directed by Josef von Sternberg, a young Austrian, is to be presented at the Mark Strand this week. This is the film which caught the fancy of Charles Chaplin, Douglas Fairbanks and Mary Pickford. Mr. Chaplin was particularly enthusiastic about the picture." At the end of the year Anabel Lane of *Film Mercury* included THE SALVATION HUNTERS in her 1925 ten-best list—below D. W. Griffith's

ISN'T LIFE WONDERFUL, King Vidor's THE BIG PARADE, Erich von Stroheim's GREED, Sven Gade's SIEGE, Augusto Genina's CYRANO DE BERGERAC, Clarence Badger's PATHS TO PARADISE, and F. W. Murnau's THE LAST LAUGH, but above Herbert Brenon's PETER PAN and Malcolm St. Clair's ARE PARENTS PEOPLE?

THE SALVATION HUNTERS is not only the first film to bear Josef von Sternberg's name as director, it is also his most explicitly personal work until the emotional recapitulation of ANATAHAN closed his career nearly thirty years later. Thus his strengths and weaknesses can be evaluated from the very beginning, long before the distractions of Dietrich and the puffery of Paramount distort the implications of his images. Most film historians, particularly those in the English-speaking world, have discussed THE SALVATION HUNTERS as a depressing descent to the lower depths in the manner of Erich von Stroheim's GREED. The fact that Sternberg's film ran for less than a week in New York and did unspectacular business elsewhere in the country only enhanced its reputation for revealing the director's initial impulse toward unglamorous realism. Assuming Sternberg's later career had not been noteworthy, THE SALVATION HUNTERS would probably be remembered, if at all, as an isolated island of integrity in a sea of Hollywood compromise. Rightly or wrongly, William K. Howard's WHITE GOLD, Karl Brown's STARK LOVE, and Robert Florey's THE LIFE AND DEATH OF A HOLLYWOOD EXTRA achieved this reputation in the twenties.

Fortunately, however, a print of THE SALVATION HUNTERS has survived so that we may revaluate the film with more historical perspective. Back in 1925, Sternberg could be criticized in terms of the way the cinema had been evolving in the acknowledged classics of that era. Sternberg's players are relatively stiff and stylized in comparison with those of Griffith, Chaplin and Lubitsch. Where Murnau needed only one title in THE LAST LAUGH, Sternberg overloads THE SALVATION HUNTERS with innumerable inserts which frequently comment on the plot without either clarifying or advancing it. Nor does Sternberg exhibit Stroheim's flair for ironic detail in GREED, particularly in that film's famous wedding scene featuring a funeral procession through the window dourly.

Even without reference to the classics of its time, THE SALVATION HUNTERS is full of discernible defects. The story jumps too abruptly from the barge to the bordello, and the two locales, visually and geologically unrelated to each other, seem to belong to two different movies. (The film was actually shot on location at San Pedro, in Chinatown, the San Fernando Valley, and at Grand-Asher Studios.) Some of Sternberg's symbols are rather awkwardly applied, none more so than the diabolically designed bull's-horns hat rack into which the malignant Man slips his head time and again to produce a kind of do-it-yourself satanic simile. Because the budget does not allow for a boom, Sternberg is forced to cut more than he would normally. The pacing is uneven, and the rendering of action, never the director's strong point, is often clumsily executed.

Yet oddly enough, THE SALVATION HUNTERS is a modern film in a way that GREED, THE GOLD RUSH, THE LAST LAUGH and even POTEMKIN are not. What has always seemed oblique and obscure in Sternberg's art as compared with that of his contemporaries is the director's reluctance to reveal everything about his characters. On the purely visual level, this reluctance is expressed through veils and filters. On the dramatic plane, Sternberg has generally avoided the kind of direct confrontations in which characters spell out all their motivations. Consequently, there is usually more to Sternberg's characters than meets the eye, and after the advent of talkies, the ear. Some of Sternberg's severer critics have written off the director's pregnant pauses and silences as meaningless mystification and obfuscation. Such criticism seemed more plausible in the twenties and thirties when themes of ennui and alienation were less fashionable than they are today. As it is, the characters in THE SALVATION HUNTERS now seem far less socially abysmal than asocially absurd in the parlance of Beckett's Theatre of the Absurd. And why? Simply because Sternberg has always been interested less in men and their societies than in men and women, or more precisely, in man's confrontation of the myths of womanhood, the underlying theme of Sternbergian cinema from THE SALVATION HUNTERS to ANATAHAN.

One of the most curious characters in the film is The Gentleman as played by Stuart Holmes, at the time the most highly-paid performer in Sternberg's poverty row cast. The Gentleman is enticed into the bordello by The Man (Otto Matiesen) who seeks to prod The Girl (Georgia Hale) into prostitution. It is not hard to imagine how Stroheim or Eisenstein would have treated this agent of socio-sexual exploitation. Close-ups of leering eyes and drooling lips would have been mandatory in the name of "satire." Not so with Sternberg. The Gentleman never loses his dignity or bearing. He is quite eager to sleep with The Girl, but he respects her reluctance, particularly when he discovers that she is driven by hunger and her concern for The Boy (George K. Arthur) and The Child (Bruce Guerin) with whom she is staying. The Gentleman acts with grace and gallantry throughout, and there is never the slightest trace of contempt or sanctimonious self-righteousness toward The Girl. Nor is he motivated by shame and guilt. The same tasteful discrimination that makes him desire The Girl makes him take enough of a liking to her to give her money for food and ask nothing in return. The civilized complexity of Sternberg's Gentleman is actually far more advanced for its time than even Adolphe Menjou's predatory Men of the World in Chaplin's A WOMAN OF PARIS and Lubitsch's THE MARRIAGE CIRCLE. It remains for Sternberg to create the first screen character who respects the woman he seeks to reduce to prostitution, prefiguring G. W. Pabst's sophisticated treatment of Louise Brooks and her respectful lovers in DIARY OF A LOST GIRL and PANDORA'S BOX later in the twenties.

Sternberg's awe toward feminine knowingness is suggested by a curiously inconsistent plot device in THE SALVATION HUNTERS. When we are first introduced to Georgia Hale, we are told in a title that she has sunk as low as her stockings, and we see a shot of her drooping stockings as visual verification. The actress, later used by Chaplin in THE GOLD RUSH as one of his few demimondaine heroines, displays here what Sternberg himself describes as "sullen charm." She is neither a forlorn waif nor a painted woman, but a girl both tired and tenacious. When The Brute (Olaf Hytten) offers her a cigarette and places his hand on her arm, she accepts the cigarette and glares at the offending hand until The Brute removes it. Meanwhile The Boy is a walking metaphor of faintheartedness and futility, and there they all are on this barge bearing a mud-dredge which scoops out earth from the water only to have its efforts cyclically negated by the compensating collapse of the shore in the background.

When The Brute begins beating an orphan child whose parents were lost to the dredge, The Girl shames The Boy into action. After a few steps of cowardly choreography, The Boy manages to drag The Child away. When The Brute gives chase, The Girl looks up meaningfully to the control booth of the dredge and signals someone we will never meet. The iron claws of the mud-scoop open above The Brute, drenching him with mud and delaying him long enough to allow The Boy and The Child, and, with them, The Girl, to "escape" from the barge to the city.

Sternberg's titles are no help here. By what power or influence did a girl "as low as her stockings" intervene so decisively in the affairs of others? From this moment of intervention, The Girl will possess a mystical authority over the life of The Boy, and it is this authority which marks Sternberg's attitude toward women long before the debut of Marlene Dietrich. In fact, the haunting image of Georgia Hale standing before a mirror to apply the blacking from a burnt-out match to her eyebrows anticipates the narcissistic mirror mystique of Ingmar Bergman by decades. The real drama of THE SALVATION HUNTERS is not concerned with the rise of the downtrodden, but rather with the moving (emotion in motion) spectacle of a Girl waiting for a Boy to grow up into a Man.

1925 THE EXQUISITE SINNER (Metro-Goldwyn-Mayer) Directed by Josef von Sternberg; later reshot in part by Philip Rosen. Script by Josef von Sternberg and Alice D. G. Miller based on the novel *Escape* by Alden Brooks. Photographed by Max Fabian. With Conrad Nagel (Dominique Prad), Renee Adoree (Gypsy Maid), Paulette Duval (Yvonne), Frank Currier (Colonel), George K. Arthur (Colonel's Orderly), Matthew Betz (Gypsy Chief), and Helene D'Algy and Claire Dubrey (Dominique's Sisters).

The collaboration between Sternberg and Mary Pickford that was to follow THE SALVATION HUNTERS never materialized. Under contract to Mary Pickford, Sternberg went to Pittsburgh to write a scenario with the city as background, and returned with a story for a subjective camera experiment (BACKWASH) in which the actress would play a blind girl and Chaplin himself would cavort grotesquely in her mind. Mary Pickford rejected the project and turned instead to a more conventional film under Marshall Neilan's direction.

Of Sternberg's ensuing work at Metro, little remains except a record of controversy. Robert Florey, his assistant on the first Metro film, THE EXQUISITE SINNER, describes the director's Teutonic tantrums in *Hollywood d'Hier et d'Aujourd'hui* in terms that make him seem like a second Stroheim. Since there is no known print of THE EXQUISITE SINNER in existence, it is difficult to determine what its significance may have been in Sternberg's career. The story, involving a rich boy who runs away from home to join a band of gypsies, seems standard for the period rather than personally Sternbergian.

The director himself seems to disown the film with ambiguous irony: "No one," he writes in his autobiography, "except a few curiously discerning friends, thought the film of any value, and as the organization had provided story and actors, it was evident that only my part in this venture had been ineffective. With unprecedented kindness, wishing to show where I had gone astray, this great organization, loaded with talent, that stumbled over itself, remade the entire film in order to make a practical demonstration of how I should have directed it. The result was two ineffective films instead of one."

The critic John Grierson had a somewhat more favorable recollection: "I knew Sternberg just after his SALVATION HUNTERS and liked him immensely," Grierson wrote in the early thirties. "He had made a fine picture for Metro called THE EXQUISITE SINNER and had been heaved off the payroll for adding some genuine local color to a Breton scene." Also despite Sternberg's misgivings, THE EXQUISITE SINNER was selected by the National Board of Review as one of the forty best pictures of 1926.

Sternberg's second Metro film project, THE MASKED BRIDE with Mae Murray, terminated abruptly when he turned his camera toward the ceiling and walked off the set after the first few days of shooting. Veteran director Christy Cabanne who finished the film quite properly received sole directorial credit.

1926 THE SEA GULL (A WOMAN OF THE SEA) Directed and written by Josef von Sternberg. Photographed by Paul Ivano. Sets by Danny Hall. Produced by Charles Chaplin. With Edna Purviance, Eve Southern, and Gane Whitman.

After his misadventures at Metro, Sternberg contracted with Charles Chaplin to direct Edna Purviance in her "comeback." Curtis Harrington has synopsized this lost film in his index of the director's work: "A simple, quadrangular love story," he writes, "served as the basis for this film in which the changing patterns of the sea were used for psychological and atmospheric underscoring of the action, photographed largely on the sea coast of Monterey, California." According to Harrington, the film was previewed once in Beverly Hills and then permanently suppressed by Chaplin. In his biography of Sternberg, Herman G. Weinberg adds that Chaplin subsequently destroyed the negative but gives no reason for such emphatic action. Chaplin does not mention Sternberg or THE SEA GULL in his autobiography, and Sternberg himself fails to throw any light on the episode.

Again the sole critical opinion is that of John Grierson, who wrote: "I watched Sternberg make still another picture, THE WOMAN OF THE SEA, for Chaplin. The story was Chaplin's, and humanist to a degree: with fishermen that toiled, and sweated, and lived and loved as proletarians do. Introspective as before, Sternberg could not see the fishermen and the fish were forgotten. It would have meant something just as fine in its different way as Chaplin's version, but he went on to doubt himself. He wanted to be a success, and here plainly and pessimistically was the one way to be unsuccessful. The film as a result was neither Chaplin's version nor Sternberg's. It was a strangely beautiful and empty affair—possibly the most beautiful I have ever seen—of net patterns, sea patterns and hair in the wind. When a director dies, he becomes a photographer."

Ultimately, the mystery of THE SEA GULL may have to do less with Sternberg's relation to Chaplin than with Chaplin's relationship with Edna Purviance. And Sternberg may have had the latter in mind in this curiously cryptic passage from his autobiography: "One of the stars consigned to my care in a film that never saw the light of day was the most willing woman that ever faced my camera. But unfortunately, when the camera turned, her face disintegrated, her eyes became helpless, and her body trembled like the leaf of an aspen. The only remedy for this condition was alcohol, which had caused it, and this was unsuitable. I called for a pair of kettledrums, and the timpani distracted her long enough for her to play her part. It was her last film and almost my last."

1927 UNDERWORLD (Famous Players-Lasky-Paramount) Directed by Josef von Sternberg. Produced by Hector Turnbull. Script by Robert N. Lee based on a story by Ben Hecht. Photographed by Bert Glennon. Sets by Hans Dreier. Titles by George Marion, Jr. With George Bancroft ("Bull" Weed), Evelyn Brent ("Feathers" McCoy), Clive Brook ("Rolls Royce"), Larry Semon ("Slippy" Lewis), Fred Kohler (Buck Mulligan), Helen Lynch (Mulligan's Girl), and Jerry Mandy (Paloma).

In Hollywood, the saying goes you are only as good as your last picture. When that has been shelved desperate measures are called for; and at the risk of fatally losing face, Sternberg accepted a job at Paramount as assistant director to Arthur Rosson. After a week, however, Paramount production chief B. P. Schulberg assigned him to do retakes on Frank Lloyd's CHILDREN OF DIVORCE with Clara Bow, Gary Cooper, and Esther Ralston, and the excellence of his salvage work earned him a project of his own. The result was UNDERWORLD, the first famous gangster film. Like THE SALVATION HUNTERS it achieved fame overnight; but unlike the earlier film its success manifested itself in public screenings at the New York Paramount and soon an all night schedule was improvised to accommodate unexpected crowds that flocked to an attraction lacking in advance publicity.

The popular success of UNDERWORLD undoubtedly established Sternberg in the Hollywood system, but the film's reputation is as misleading as that of THE SALVATION HUNTERS. Film histories generally treat UNDERWORLD as a crisp, crackling melodrama that races along to a devastating dénouement, and despite stylistic aberrations like Rouben Mamoulian's CITY STREETS, this is what we have come to expect from the gangster genre over the years. However, UNDERWORLD is less a proto-gangster film than a pre-gangster film.

George Bancroft's "Bull" Weed is Sternberg's Byronic hero, preceding later gangsters more in the manner of poetic prophecy than of journalistic observation. Sternberg's hoodlums, like Cocteau's motorcyclists in ORPHÉE, partake of the manners and machinery of the modern world without ever escaping from the dream world of their creator. The avenging forces of law and order are never related to society but rather to an implacable Fate which awaits every tragic hero. In this sense, UNDERWORLD unfolds from the point of view of the gangster and is the first in a tradition which has included LITTLE CAESAR, THE PUBLIC ENEMY, SCAR-FACE, HIGH SIERRA, WHITE HEAT, THE ASPHALT JUN-GLE, THEY LIVE BY NIGHT, and THE KILLING, as well as PEPE LE MOKO and GRISBI.

The fact that Ben Hecht was connected with the scripts of both UNDERWORLD and SCARFACE (directed by Howard Hawks) has led some film historians to establish a direct link between the two films, but it is interesting also to trace the divergence of direction between Sternberg and Hawks. Hawks, of course, enjoyed obvious advantages in dealing with a well-developed genre in 1932 instead of improvising in an unexplored subject area as Sternberg did five years earlier. The sound of gunfire in the later film was more effective than the sight of gunsmoke in its silent predecessor, and Paul Muni's "Scarface" was based on the documented reality of Al Capone, whereas George Bancroft's UNDERWORLD mobster seemed to spring solely from Sternberg's imagination.

In fact, Sternberg showed little interest in the purely gangsterish aspects of the genre, and his civilized characters consistently transcend the criminal codes of Hawks and Hecht. It is instructive, for example, to compare Sternberg's treatment of Evelyn Brent in UNDERWORLD with Hawks' treatment of Louise Brooks in A GIRL IN EVERY PORT. Where Louise Brooks becomes the "heavy" for breaking up the beautiful relationship between Victor McLaglen and Edmund Lowe, Evelyn Brent emerges in UNDERWORLD as the glittering protagonist, a beacon for male revenge and redemption. There is no suggestion in Sternberg's film as there is in SCARFACE that women are perversely attracted to men of violence. Where Karen Morley's

eyes light up with manic glee when she realizes Paul Muni will become her new lover simply because he has eliminated his predecessor, Evelyn Brent falls in love with Clive Brook only when she recognizes the seriousness of his personality.

Typically, Sternberg's UNDERWORLD characters make up in depth and ambiguity what they lack in detail and verisimilitude. Evelyn Brent's "Feathers" McCoy, festooned in fluffy down from head to toe, is a uniquely Sternbergian creation, and her drunken coronation during the Walpurgisnacht of the gangsters' ball places the director in his most persuasive milieu. There, where streams of confetti trace a mockingly merry pattern against the moodily filtered lights and shadows, Sternberg's underworld is visually rendered as a hell of false illusions.

Sternberg has never been particularly fond of UN-DERWORLD as an example of personal expression; perhaps the charges of commercialism leveled against it have colored his judgment. Despite his expressed preference for THE SALVATION HUNTERS as reflecting his personality, it can be argued that there is more of his poetry in UNDERWORLD. The performances are memorable if uneven, and there is a wealth of creative gesture for even the most minor characterization. Sternberg can develop his plot within a frame simply by varying the way George Bancroft reacts to Clive Brook's unyielding poise. No director in the history of the cinema can match Sternberg's preoccupation with the harmonies of hand signals. This realm is usually restricted to actors only, but Sternberg ignored the tabu at his own peril. To light a cigarette, to grasp a coffee cup, to fondle one's furs is, for Sternberg, equivalent to baring one's soul.

The pattern for a recurring duality of male types is established here with the clash of George Bancroft's hulking Caliban and Clive Brook's weary Prospero. Emil Jannings and William Powell in THE LAST COM-MAND and Gary Cooper and Adolphe Menjou in MOROCCO are later manifestations of Sternberg's contrasting conceptions of masculinity.

Some film historians have traced UNDERWORLD as the beginning of Sternberg's compromise with the Hollywood system. Others honor the film for initiating

UNDERWORLD (1927). Clive Brook

UNDERWORLD (1927). George Bancroft and Evelyn Brent

a promising pre-Dietrich series of stylistic experiments. Most meaningfully perhaps, Sternberg steers clear of the sociological implications of his material to concentrate on the themes which most obsess him and his heroes: love, and faith, and falsehood.

1928 THE LAST COMMAND (Paramount)

Directed by Josef von Sternberg. Script by
John F. Goodrich, from an original story by
Sternberg, based on an incident told by Ernst
Lubitsch to Lajos Biro. Sets by Hans Dreier.
Photographed by Bert Glennon. Titles by Herman J.
Mankiewicz. With Emil Jannings (Sergius
Alexander), Evelyn Brent (Natacha), William
Powell (Leo), Nicholas Soussanin (The Adjutant),
and Michael Visaroff (Serge the Valet).

The writing credits are somewhat controversial.
I have used Harrington's credit list, if only as the
most inclusive, though there seems to be something
of Bunbury in Biro since, quite recently, Robert
Graves remarked in a BBC documentary on the
ill-fated production of I, CLAUDIUS that "Lajos Biro"
had been commissioned to do the screenplay. In
this context, "Lajos Biro" is quite obviously a
pseudonym for Josef von Sternberg.

The prestige of UNDERWORLD led Paramount executives to keep Sternberg occupied, and in the next three years he directed THE LAST COMMAND, THE DRAG NET, THE DOCKS OF NEW YORK, THE CASE OF LENA SMITH, and THUNDERBOLT. In the same period, he also found time to write the scenario for Mauritz Stiller's THE STREET OF SIN, and to work on the cutting of Erich von Stroheim's THE WEDDING MARCH.

Sternberg's first assignment after UNDERWORLD was to direct Emil Jannings, the eminent German star Paramount had imported to join Ernst Lubitsch and Pola Negri in Hollywood. The film Sternberg made with Jannings was generally considered the best of Jannings' brief American career, surpassing even Ernst Lubitsch's THE PATRIOT and Victor Fleming's THE WAY OF ALL FLESH.

THE LAST COMMAND is undoubtedly Sternberg's most Pirandellian film. The director has laid claim to the plot despite the official credit assigned to Lajos Biro. The late Preston Sturges called THE LAST COMMAND just about the only perfect film he had ever seen, and both Sternberg and Emil Jannings were amply honored at the time for their participation in the production. This is the only time in his career that Sternberg confronts his own craft as a subject, his camera as an object. The story of a Czarist general reduced to the role of a Hollywood extra would seem to be a natural for both Sternberg and Jannings. Jannings, particularly, spent most of his career in sagas of decline and downfall, and he possessed the bulk, if not always the stature, for the most sordid tragedy. Here he savors every moment of authority granted to him by the texture of his fur-lined military overcoat and the aggressive angle of the cigarette holder clenched between his teeth. He is also sensually arrogant toward Evelyn Brent's Red Agent, and this we know by now constitutes the hubris of Sternbergian cinema. Jannings is humbled for his arrogance, not once but twice. Not only does the Revolution strip away the insignias of his rank, but he ends in Hollywood with a parody of his former power.

Some critics have complained about the excessive contrivance of William Powell's character, that of the Red Revolutionary turned Hollywood director. Key relationships and motivations are either unexplained or undeveloped, and the titles often fail to express the nuances of the expressions exchanged between the

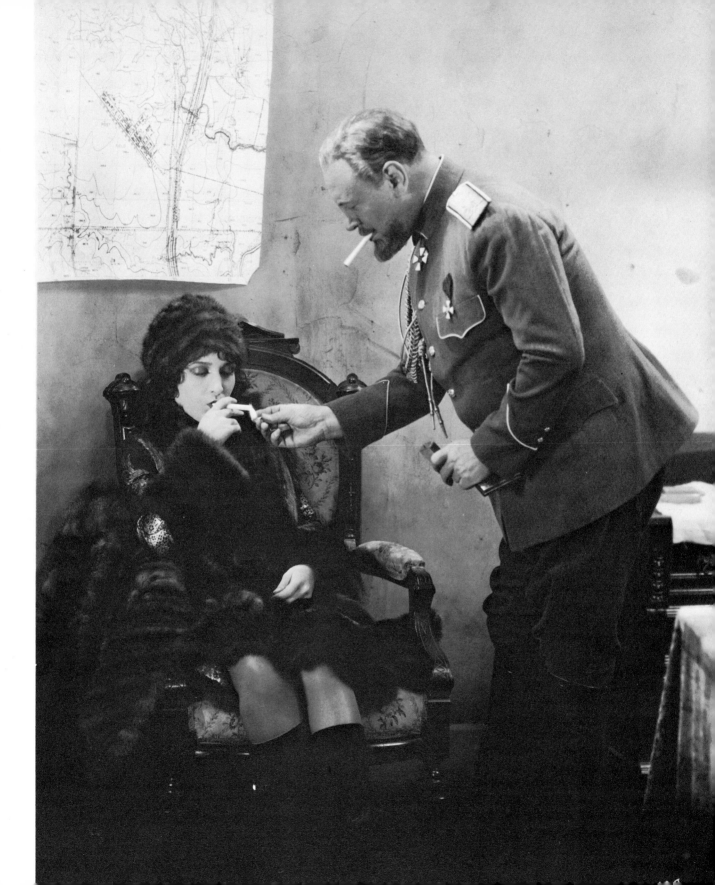

principals. The apparent train-crash death of the Evelyn Brent character seems illogical in terms of plot construction though rumor has it that a subsequent scene with Brent wound up on the cutting room floor. We never know to what extent, if any, Powell's humiliation of Jannings is motivated by Brent's fate. We are left only with the stirring spectacle of Jannings' insanity, and Powell's ambiguous compassion. There is probably a bit of Sternberg in both Jannings and Powell, as both the victim and the poet of folly.

Sternberg's formal control of his material can be illustrated by a comparison of the angle at which Jannings reviews his troops at the beginning of the film with the angle at which Powell reviews his extras at the end. Where Jannings moves laterally from left to right, Powell moves semi-vertically from right to left. The tempo is increased perceptibly for Powell's review, and this is as it should be for this musical aspect of cinema. Sternberg's technique thus exhibits a formal memory, and his "poetry," far from being vaguely disorganized in the currently pejorative sense of the "poetic," is actually a kind of visual versification.

Again Sternberg eschews the relentless expressiveness of some of his contemporaries, and it becomes impossible to tell what THE LAST COMMAND means. Evelyn Brent's relationship to Jannings is as complex as anything in the modern cinema. She seems fascinated by his power, and yet when he is completely helpless, she is not without pity and compassion. Evelyn Brent, like all Sternbergian women, remains enigmatic beyond the demands of the plot. Her perverse nature operates beyond good and evil, beyond the convenient categories of virgins and vamps. What is unusual about Sternberg's direction of his players is that, unlike Murnau and Stroheim, he seeks to control performances not for the sake of simplicity but for the sake of complexity. For example, we assume from the plot that Powell chooses Jannings for the climactic charge mainly to humiliate his former adversary, but we are never entirely sure that Powell is not motivated also by an inspiration of ideal casting. The personal, the political, the aesthetic are all intertwined influences for Sternberg. We are left then with no moral, no message, but an only partially resolved melodrama of pride and punishment, a work of art rich in overtones but pitched at too many different keys of interpretation. As a stylistic exercise, THE LAST COMMAND is almost too much of a good thing.

THE LAST COMMAND (1928). Evelyn Brent, opposite, and with Emil Jannings, preceding page

1928 THE DRAG NET (Famous Players-Lasky-Paramount) Directed by Josef von Sternberg. Script by Jules and Charles Furthman based on the story "Nightstick" by Oliver H. P. Garrett. Photographed by Harold Rosson. Sets by Hans Dreier. Titles by Herman J. Mankiewicz. With George Bancroft ("Two-Gun" Nolan), Evelyn Brent ("The Magpie"), William Powell ("Dapper" Frank Trent), Fred Kohler ("Gabby" Steve), Francis MacDonald ("Sniper" Dawson), and Leslie Fenton (Donovan).

There is no known print of THE DRAG NET in existence. Most film historians dismiss the film as a secondary, if stylish, follow-up to UNDERWORLD, and the plot does sound excessively contrived—George Bancroft's detective character, "Two Gun" Nolan wresting Evelyn Brent's "Magpie" from William Powell's "Dapper" Frank Trent of the underworld. In the course of confetti-strewn action, Bancroft is framed, Brent wounded, and Powell killed, and Bancroft gets Brent at the fade-out. Plots, however, are no clue to the merits of Sternberg's films, and until this long-missing film materializes, we must suspend judgment on a work that bridges THE LAST COMMAND and THE DOCKS OF NEW YORK. It might be noted in passing that Sternberg's "drag net" is still two words as opposed to Jack Webb's one word "Dragnet." Police parlance was still dripping wet in Sternberg's time, and the drag net had not yet shaken off the metaphoric fish in its folds.

1929 THE DOCKS OF NEW YORK (Famous Players-Lasky-Paramount) Directed by Josef von Sternberg. Script by Jules Furthman suggested by "The Dockwalloper" by John Monk Saunders. Photographed by Harold Rosson. Sets by Hans Dreier. Titles by Julian Johnson. With George Bancroft (Bill Roberts), Betty Compson (Sadie), Olga Baclanova (Lou), Clyde Cook ("Sugar" Steve), Mitchell Lewis (Third Engineer), Gustav von Seyffertitz ("Hymn Book" Harry), Lillian Worth (Steve's Girl), Guy Oliver (The Crimp), and May Foster (Mrs. Crimp).

THE DOCKS OF NEW YORK, released toward the end of the silent era, quickly vanished into undeserved obliv-ion. Seen today, it confirms Chaplin's observation that the silent movies had learned their craft just about the time they went out of business. William K. Everson, the encyclopedic expert on the silent film, has noted that THE DOCKS OF NEW YORK and Paul Fejos' legendary LONESOME were previewed for the New York press the same week as the Al Jolson vehicle, THE SINGING FOOL, and the two sensitive silent films were completely passed over in the frenzied clamor over Jolson's maudlin song-fest.

More than in any previous film, Sternberg has integrated spectacle with psychology, and his characters gain in clarity what they lose in complexity. Sternberg's direction of his players has never been more controlled as George Bancroft, Betty Compson, Olga Baclanova, and Gustav von Seyffertitz perform with force and subtlety as denizens of the lower depths. Sternberg's facility with the shifting moods of the film is equally remarkable. From the Hogarthian hullabaloo of a Walpurgisnacht in a dockside saloon to the glum remorse and resignation of the morning after in magistrate's court, Sternberg's camera finds the proper angle and distance. His final image of Betty Compson in a crowded courtroom in long-shot, objectively anonymous but subjectively heroic, reveals a mastery of the expressive potentialities of the focal length of the lens.

George Bancroft is once more Sternberg's Caliban, but Betty Compson's fatalistic floozie is more prone to wearing her heart on her sleeve than most Sternbergian heroines. She is vulnerable, wistful, yet fully committed in the way Sylvia Sidney will be later in AN AMERICAN TRAGEDY. The plot is something of a switch for Sternberg in that it is the man who deludes the woman, first with a mock wedding and then with a cynical honeymoon. The man satisfies his lust, but then surrenders to his conscience.

Sternberg quietly dramatizes the emotional transition with a scene in which Compson sews Bancroft's pocket after it has been torn by Bancroft's jealous buddy. This pocket, like Desdemona's handkerchief, becomes the visual correlative of the drama, the battleground between conjugal feelings and fraternal loyalties. To emphasize the stakes in this struggle, Sternberg even shifts from an objective to a subjective camera viewpoint by photographing out-of-focus the needle Compson tries to thread through her tears. When Bancroft

1152-4

takes the needle away and threads it himself, the domestic irony of the situation takes on a new dimension. It becomes psychologically clear through this external gesture that Bancroft needs Compson's love more than her care, and that, conversely, Compson has more love in her than care. Bancroft's final decision to return to Compson is thus more a rising to an occasion than a settling down to a situation, and Bancroft rises literally, visually, from the subterranean caverns of his ship, up the ladder to the sunlit deck and then over the side into the purifying waters, clambering back to the shore like the creatures of old instinctively seeking their ulitmate humanity on the evolutionary ladder.

With THE DOCKS OF NEW YORK, Sternberg takes his place with the directors of camera movement as opposed to the directors of montage. In one continuous flow across his décor, Sternberg shows Bancroft dragging his would-be bride past a universe of drunken revelers. The emphasis is on the movement itself rather than on its destination, or rather on the carnal passion expressed by the slow relentlessness of the movement. The language of Sternberg's camera movement here is not the language of dreams, but the language of immediacy. Now, now, now, Bancroft seems to shout visually with each lumbering step, and the insinuating insistence of Sternberg's slow tempo augments the electrifying effect of the spectacle.

Sternberg's slow dissolves in THE DOCKS OF NEW YORK have been noted by some film historians as symptoms of stylistic self-indulgence when, actually, they serve the same function as Godard's jump cuts in BREATHLESS, and that is to indicate the meaninglessness of the time intervals between moral decisions. When time becomes a function of melodramatic action and reaction in the course of events leading up to Olga Baclanova's murdering her unfaithful mate, Sternberg's cutting is as crisp and clean as Fritz Lang's. Not until MOROCCO did Sternberg employ slow dissolves for symbolic linkage, and even then and after he used them more sparingly than did George Stevens, the poet laureate of the slow dissolve after A PLACE IN THE SUN.

Sternberg is no more realistic than he has ever been, but his characters are on the whole far more plausible

THE DOCKS OF NEW YORK (1928). Betty Compson and George Bancroft above, Olga Baclanova below. Courtesy George Eastman House

THE DOCKS OF NEW YORK (1928). Betty Compson and George Bancroft. Courtesy George Eastman House

than Stroheim's. Stroheim's reputation as a realist is based almost entirely on GREED, a film peopled exclusively by grotesque gargoyles. Without dwelling on the details of poverty, Sternberg, like Chaplin, can look at the poor in terms of a life style of survival. A wooden match, after all, can be ignited with as much physical grace as a solid gold cigarette lighter. By contrast, Stroheim looks at anyone beneath the aristocracy as positively horrid and vulgar, and the aristocracy itself as absurdly depraved (sentimentalized heroines, of course, excluded). Stroheim is thus more a satirist than a realist, in the manner of Buñuel and Chabrol more a surrealist than a realist.

At first glance, Sternberg seems more like Visconti, a prettifier of poverty, except that Sternberg, unlike Visconti, never claims to be realistic. His photography, full of light and shadow, is designed to give visual expression more to feelings than to facts. He is not concerned with social conditions on the docks of New York, nor with the class consciousness of his characters. What interests him is the emotional force which impels a man to drag a woman across a crowded room to satisfy his desires, and that emotional force can be expressed in one manner and one manner alone: camera movement. Sternberg wants to drag us along with Miss Compson, and he succeeds, and then he shows us Miss Compson overcoming all this brute force, and we realize that we are back in the realm of Sternberg's feminine mystique. With DOCKS OF NEW YORK, Sternberg takes his place with D. W. Griffith and Frank Borzage as one of Hollywood's least condescending chroniclers of little people with big emotions. Sternberg stands alone, however, for his unique virtuousness untainted by sanctimoniousness.

1929 THE CASE OF LENA SMITH

(Famous-Players-Lasky-Paramount) Directed by Josef von Sternberg. Script by Jules Furthman based on a story by Samuel Ornitz. Titles by Julian Johnson. Photographed by Harold Rosson. Sets by Hans Dreier. With Esther Ralston (Lena Smith), James Hall (Franz Hofrat), Gustav von Seyffertitz (Herr Hofrat), Emily Fitzroy (Frau Hofrat), Fred Kohler (Stefan), Betty Aho (Stefan's sister), Lawrence Grant (Commissioner), Alex Woloshin (Janitor), Ann Brody (Janitor's wife),

and Lola Lane, Kay Deslys, Warner Klinger, and Wally Albright, Jr.

There is no known print of THE CASE OF LENA SMITH in existence, and this is doubly unfortunate because it appears to have been more personal than THE EXQUISITE SINNER and more unusual than THE DRAG NET. Since it is the only film in which Sternberg directed Esther Ralston, its absence also prevents us from assigning her a place in his gallery of heroines. The story seems to have impressed both John Grierson and Curtis Harrington as possessing more substance than was usual with Sternberg projects; and while one must always be wary of Grierson bearing gifts to Sternberg, the stills are intriguing.

The prologue and epilogue of the film occur during the First World War, but the main part of the narrative is set in the Vienna of 1894, the place and time of Sternberg's birth. Consequently, THE CASE OF LENA SMITH, in both mood and milieu may well be Sternberg's one overt memory film. The plot concerns a peasant girl who comes to Vienna, where she secretly marries a dissolute army officer, bears his child, and then becomes a servant in his father's home. The dénouement involves her defiance of the father when he tries to take her child.

One cannot begin calculating the childhood traumas that could have fed this anecdote. Recalling one of the film's most admired sequences in his autobiography, Sternberg savors the vividness of the original experience: "Mine was every crevice of the vast amusement park, the like of which never again existed. . . . Hundreds of shooting galleries, Punch and Judy and the inevitable Satan puppet, chalk-faced clowns in their dominoes, boats sliding from a high point down into water with a great splash, leather-faced dummies that groaned when slapped, pirouetting fleas, sword swallowers, tumbling midgets and men on stilts, contortionists, jugglers and acrobats, wild swings with skirts flaring from them, proving that not all females had lost their undergarments, a forest of balloons, tattooed athletes, muscle-bulging weight lifters, women who were sawed in half and apparently spent the rest of their lives truncated, trained dogs and elephants, tightropes that provided footing for a gourmet who feasted on a basketful of the local sausages with horse-radish that made my mouth water, graceful ballerinas, grunting knife throwers with screaming targets whose hair flowed down to the hems of their nightgowns, hatchet-throwing Indians and phlegmatic squaws, double-headed calves, members of the fair sex, fat and bearded, with thighs that could pillow an army, magicians who poured jugs of flaming liquid down their throats, drum-thumping cannibals and their wiggling harems, a glass maze from which the delighted customers stumbled with black eyes and gashed heads, hypnotists who practised levitation and passed hoops around the dormant females swaying five feet from where they ought to have been, and the central figure of a huge Chinese mandarin with drooping mustaches longer than the tail of a horse revolving on a merry-go-round to the tune of Ivanovici's *Donauwellen*—and what more could I have asked?"

1929 THUNDERBOLT (Famous Players-Lasky-Paramount) Directed by Josef von Sternberg. Adapted by Charles Furthman from a story by Jules and Charles Furthman. Dialogue by Herman J. Mankiewicz. Photography by Henry Gerrard. Sets by Hans Dreier. With George Bancroft ("Thunderbolt"), Richard Arlen (Bob Moran), Fay Wray ("Ritzy"), Tully Marshall (Warden), Eugenie Besserer (Mrs. Moran), James Spottswood ("Snapper" O'Shea), Fred Kohler ("Bad Al" Frieberg), Mike Donlin ("Kentucky" Sampson), S. S. Stewart (Negro Convict), George Irving (Bank Officer), Robert Elliott (Priest), William Thorne (Police Inspector), and E. H. Calvert (District Attorney).

Like UNDERWORLD before it, THUNDERBOLT is less a gangster film than a gangster fantasy. Its speech is stylized, its noise of gunfire muted. THUNDERBOLT is generally overlooked when film historians evaluate Sternberg's contributions to the early sound film. Although 1929 is cited as the year of Lubitsch's THE LOVE PARADE, Vidor's HALLELUJAH! and Mamoulian's APPLAUSE, Sternberg fails to come in for mention until THE BLUE ANGEL and MOROCCO launch him into sound and song in 1930. Nonetheless, THUNDERBOLT is, in retrospect, a startling experiment with the kind of asynchronous sound that Eisenstein and Pudovkin were issuing manifestos about at the time.

Sternberg is particularly resourceful in THUNDERBOLT in his use of sound and music for mood effects, and the very unreality of his style seems to justify the unusual density of his sound track. An indication of what really interests him is given in a scene that employs sound contrapuntally. When George Bancroft flees a police raid on a Harlem bar, the guns chatter offscreen but the camera remains focused on and hypnotized by Fay Wray clutching her furs as she sits alone at the table. For Sternberg, it is the woman who counts even during a crucial chase in what is supposed to be a gangster movie.

Throughout his career Sternberg refused to recognize that sound was exercising a naturalistic influence in the cinema. Audiences reacted to speech on the screen more for its prosaic immediacy than for its poetic imaginativeness. The ideal for dialogue was crisp currency rather than contrived cadences, and thus the player's tempo generally prevailed over the director's. (PUBLIC ENEMY is speeded up more by James Cagney than William Wellman, just as CITY STREETS is slowed down more by Gary Cooper than Rouben Mamoulian.) Sternberg resisted the heresy of acting autonomy to the very end of his career, and that resistance is very likely one of the reasons his career was foreshortened.

The world that he created in THUNDERBOLT was a private one visually, as well as aurally. When the police question Fay Wray about her hoodlum lover they mount her on a raised platform where she sits in star-like splendor caressing her furs. Subsequent gangster movies fostered a far different impression of the third degree as imagination gave way to observation. Nor is Sternberg unduly concerned with plot probability. The frame-up of Richard Arlen on a murder charge is a ridiculously facile contrivance even for Sternberg, and it is obvious that his only interest is in the bar-shadowed spectacle of Richard Arlen and George Bancroft in opposite cells on Death Row, two doomed men thinking about the same girl. Once the preposterous machinery is accepted, the plot proceeds to its delirious dénouement with force and conviction. Sternberg is not concerned with how or why people get where they are as he is with how they act and feel once they get there. There is a fatalistic spell in Sternberg's style, and at its best, the imagery transcends the improbability.

Fay Wray's performance makes a curious contrast to

her intense ingenue in Stroheim's THE WEDDING MARCH. Where Stroheim gives her an aura of innocence the better to set off the depravity of the world around her, Sternberg mixes the sugar and spice in more equal proportions. Thus, simultaneously rather than sequentially, the same girl is both a dazzling gangster's moll and a demure bankteller's sweetheart. KING KONG cultists notwithstanding, Fay Wray was never one of the more overwhelming personalities of the American cinema, and her relative pliability makes her a meaningful manifestation of Sternberg's unified vision of Woman as both Magdalene and Madonna, a unity found also in Ophuls and Mizoguchi, but lacking in the divided vision of Ford and Visconti. (It is perhaps fitting that Dietrich's first name is a conscious fusion of Maria and Magdalene.) The family scenes of Fay Wray, Richard Arlen, and Arlen's mother, Eugenie Besserer, are played in a comfortable atmosphere of genial virtue, and although Sternberg disowns some of the film's shaggy-dog animal sentimentality, THUNDERBOLT gives him away once more as a virtuous man obsessed by the spectacle of vice.

THUNDERBOLT actually preceded HALLELUJAH!, and yet the vaguely jazz-and-blues atmosphere of a Harlem saloon and the Negro spirituals on Death Row have been almost completely ignored by the conscientious compilers of that sort of thing. THUNDERBOLT is, in some respects, as much a musical as a melodrama. Above all, George Bancroft's superhuman anticipation of death is the stuff of grand opera.

THUNDERBOLT (1929). Fay Wray and George Bancroft

1930 THE BLUE ANGEL (DER BLAUE ENGEL) (UFA-Paramount) Directed by Josef von Sternberg. Produced by Erich Pommer. Adapted by Carl Zuckmayer, Karl Vollmöller, and Robert Liebmann from the novel *Professor Unrat* by Heinrich Mann. Photographed by Günther Rittau and Hans Schneeberger. Sets by Otto Hunte. Songs: "Ich bin von Kopf bis Fuss auf Liebe eingestellt" ("Falling in Love Again"), "Ich bin die fesche Lola" ("They Call Me Naughty Lola"), "Nimm Dich in acht vor blonden Frauen," and "Kinder, heut' abend such ich mir was aus" by Friedrich Hollander (music) and Robert Liebmann (lyrics). With Emil Jannings (Professor Immanuel Rath), Marlene Dietrich (Lola Fröhlich), Kurt Gerron (Kiepert, a magician), Rosa Valetti (Guste, his wife), Hans Albers (Mazeppa), Eduard von Winterstein (Principal of the School), Reinhold Bernt (The Clown), Hans Roth (Beadle), Rolf Müller (Angst, a student), Rolant Varno (Lohman, a student), Karl Balhaus (Ertzum, a student), Robert Klein-Lörk (Goldstaub, a student), Karl Huszar-Puffy (Publican), Wilhelm Diegelmann (Captain), Gerhard Bienert (Policeman), and Ilse Fürstenberg (Rath's housekeeper).

THE BLUE ANGEL occupies a paradoxical if preeminent place in Sternberg's career. Emil Jannings reportedly requested Sternberg as the director to guide the silent star past the sound barrier, and Sternberg agreed despite a previous clash of temperaments in THE LAST COMMAND. The film was produced simultaneously in German and English language versions for the maximum benefit of the Paramount-UFA combine in world markets, and thus with this one excursion into Europe all the ambiguity of Sternberg's origins reappeared as the "von" in his name was finally vindicated. After THE BLUE ANGEL, Sternberg would once more be treated in retrospect as a European legend corrupted by Hollywood lucre.

"Camp," declared Susan Sontag in the sixties, "is the outrageous estheticism of von Sternberg's six American movies with Dietrich, all six but especially the last, THE DEVIL IS A WOMAN . . ." Significantly, Miss Sontag pointedly excludes THE BLUE ANGEL from her Camp sight. The snobbery of subtitles aside, THE BLUE ANGEL is undoubtedly the one Sternberg film the director's severest detractors will concede is beyond reproach and ridicule. It is worth noting, if only in passing, that Marlene Dietrich did not appear on American screens in THE BLUE ANGEL until after the release of MOROCCO, actually her second stint with Sternberg.

Although THE BLUE ANGEL may have been admired in some quarters for the wrong reasons, the film stands up today as Sternberg's most efficient achievement both emotionally and expressively. There are no hidden corners, no nagging nuances, no puzzling paradoxes. For once Sternberg is in complete rapport with his audience with a film that is at once his most brutal and least humorous. "In converting the novel into a film which would meet my standards of visual poetry," he recalls, "I introduced the figure of the clown as well as all the episodes and details that led the professor to be confined in a straitjacket."

The ultimately tragic irony of THE BLUE ANGEL is double-edged in a way Sternberg could not have anticipated when he undertook the project. The rise of Lola Lola and the fall of Professor Immanuel Rath in reel life is paralleled in real life by the rise of Marlene Dietrich and the fall of Emil Jannings. When THE BLUE ANGEL was revived in the early fifties, the critical consensus upheld the public on Dietrich's directness over Jannings' detailedness. The tedious tics of elaborately expressionistic acting have long since gone out of style, and there is still a tendency to underrate the Jannings performance. In the context of the screen's cuckolds, however, Jannings surpasses in tragic intensity even Raimu and Ake Groneberg. What he lacks in the style and stature of his Czarist general turned Hollywood extra in THE LAST COMMAND, he more than makes up here with the nakedness of his passion.

Sternberg's sense of tragic dignity in the midst of tawdry downfall is best illustrated at that moment when Jannings hurls himself into a room to wreak vengeance on his wife and her strong-man lover. The camera remains at a discreet angle and distance from the doorway through which Dietrich escapes. The men with the straitjacket sweep past her, but we never actually see Jannings subdued by them, only Dietrich looking with ambiguous compassion at the spectacle of subjugation. Jannings has had his moment of masculine beauty on the stage by crowing like a maddened rooster at Dietrich's deception. In that soul-stirring moment Sternberg suggests through Jannings what it is to be a man, and Sternberg will not cheapen that moment by degrading a man who has been defeated.

THE BLUE ANGEL achieves its most electrifying effects through careful grading and construction. When Marlene Dietrich sings "Falling in Love Again" for the first time the delivery is playful, flirtatious, and self-consciously seductive. The final rendition is harsher, colder, and relentlessly remorseless. The difference in delivery is not related to the old stereotype of the vamp finally showing her true colors, but rather to a psychological development in Dietrich's Lola from mere sensual passivity to a more forceful fatalism about the nature of her desires. Lola's first instinct is to accept the Professor's paternal protection and her last is to affirm her natural instincts not as coquettish expedients, but as the very terms by which she expresses her existence. Thus, as the Professor has been defeated by Lola's beauty, Lola has been ennobled by the Professor's jealousy. It is in this complex interplay that THE BLUE ANGEL transcends the trivial genre of bourgeois male corrupted by bohemian female.

The sordid atmosphere with which Sternberg embellishes his drama emphasizes the grossness to be endured in grappling with desire. On one level of characterization, the Professor is a Lazarus resurrected from a dismal fastidiousness of death-like feelings by sniffing his way through Lola's life-drenched garments, *objets d'art* less of a symbolist than a fetishist.

Setting up a scene for THE BLUE ANGEL (1930). Sternberg,
Emil Jannings, and Kurt Gerron

26

THE BLUE ANGEL (1930). Emil Jannings

Fortunately, the niggling necessities of economics intervene between the drab décor and any of its frivolously sado-masochistic implications. It is not Lola who forces the Professor to peddle her gamey photos, but rather the financial realities of the situation. The shabbiness eventually engulfs the sensuality, but it is Lola's strength that she has lived with shabbiness long enough to know how to bend without breaking, and the Professor's tragic misfortune to bend first and still to break afterward.

It is not specifically Germany or the German character with which Sternberg is concerned here, but rather the spectacle of a prudent, prudish man blocked off from all means of displaying his manhood except the most animalistic. Sternberg himself has explicitly removed THE BLUE ANGEL from the socially significant path Siegfried Kracauer has traced *From Caligari to Hitler*. Yet the fact that THE BLUE ANGEL is coincidentally Sternberg's only German-made film and his most violent work may suggest that he felt the conflict between order and nature would be more violent in a German setting than in any other. This supposition, however, does not justify the judgment that Sternberg's deliberately designed drabness reflects realistically observed details of a decadent society. The world of THE BLUE ANGEL is as much a dream world as the world of THE SALVATION HUNTERS, but the illusion of reality is much stronger in THE BLUE ANGEL because the characters are less abstract.

Jean Renoir's LA CHIENNE (1931) and Ingmar Bergman's THE NAKED NIGHT (1953) are more profound examinations of the crisis of cuckoldry in the illusion-shattering life of man, but THE BLUE ANGEL is more successful dramatically. Where Renoir is more realistic and Bergman more literary, Sternberg is more effective in resolving his tragedy within the form he has postulated for it. Renoir arbitrarily ends his film as if it were a stylized spectacle of the Paris streets, but his implication is clear: life goes on, transcending pride, passion, and morality. For Bergman life is a mystery which no amount of thought can solve. Renoir and Bergman are thus concerned with ideas beyond the frames of their films, whereas Sternberg remains within his frames. For the Professor there is only his life with Lola, and deprived of Lola there is nothing but death. There is no life for Lola and the Professor beyond the running time of THE BLUE ANGEL. There is no world beyond the outer limits of the set. Renoir and Bergman appeal to our common sense. Sternberg appeals to our sense of spectacle.

Not that Renoir and Bergman lack mood and mannerism. Far from it. Nor can we single out THE BLUE ANGEL for projecting Sternberg through Jannings. There is a great deal of Renoir in Michel Simon from LA CHIENNE, and a great deal of Bergman in Ake Groneberg from THE NAKED NIGHT. For the most part, however, LA CHIENNE and THE NAKED NIGHT open out on the world, whereas THE BLUE ANGEL turns in on itself. Sternberg's profundity is consequently measured less by the breadth of his vision than by the perfection of his form and by the emotional force of his characters within that form.

How much more painfully poignant, too, is the scene where Jannings helps Dietrich with her stockings than a similar Jannings maneuver with Lya da Putti in Du Pont's VARIETY, where Jannings as the dupe, pure and simple, is treated with amused contempt. By contrast, Dietrich's air of sensual complicity in THE BLUE ANGEL redeems the Jannings character from complete ridiculousness. There is in Sternberg a savoring of sensuality for its own sake that is both more human and more satisfying than Renoir's uncompromising humanism and Bergman's unyielding pessimism. The disassociation of Dietrich's sexuality from normal standards of dramatic psychology becomes more apparent in her later collaborations with Sternberg. In THE BLUE ANGEL, Dietrich is still somewhat submerged in her characterization and not yet completely possessed by her personality. She straddles a chair as she will later straddle a horse in THE SCARLET EMPRESS, imperiously, magisterially, fully the measurer of men in the audience, but yet she is also an organic character who finds a certain kind of maturity in marriage. If "serious" criticism of the cinema were not as puritanical as it is, the experiences of Lola and the Professor would seem more pertinent to the hidden world of domestic sexuality than is now the case. The idea that all eroticism is hopelessly exotic has made Sternbergian cinema seem much stranger than it is.

1930 MOROCCO (Paramount) Directed by Josef von Sternberg. Script by Jules Furthman based on the play *Amy Jolly* by Benno Vigny.

Photographed by Lee Garmes. Sets by Hans Dreier. Songs: "Give Me the Man" and "What Am I Bid for My Apples?" by Leo Robin (lyrics) and Karl Hajos (music); "Quand L'Amour Meurt" by Millandy and Cremieux. With Gary Cooper (Tom Brown), Marlene Dietrich (Amy Jolly), Adolphe Menjou (La Bessière), Ullrich Haupt (Adjutant Caesar), Juliette Compton (Anna Dolores), Francis MacDonald (Corporal Tatoche), Albert Conti (Colonel Quinnevières), Eve Southern (Mme. Caesar), Paul Porcasi (Impresario), Emile Chautard (French general), and Michael Visaroff.

MOROCCO revisited is a revelation to the viewer who anticipates a heavy-breathing Sardou-like safari across the desert sands. Instead, one is treated to the paradox of characters unostentatiously impulsive, expressing the most delirious feelings with the most delicate gestures. Every bit of bric-a-brac, every shadowed shutter, every fluttering fabric conveys the characters inexorably toward an emotional decision they would resist if they could. Yet if they surrender to disastrous, even faintly ridiculous impulses, they do so as undemandingly and as unobtrusively as possible. Here again a plot synopsis cannot possibly suggest the preciseness of Sternberg's sensibility. To say that a woman gives up everything for love is to oversimplify the civilized complexity of an intrigue triangulated by a café canary, a Foreign Legionnaire, and a mustachioed man of the world, a plot less written than wired for the star voltage generated by Gary Cooper, Marlene Dietrich, and Adolphe Menjou. On this latter level, MOROCCO is Sternberg's Hollywood movie par excellence.

For all its frenzied fabulousness, MOROCCO succeeded in its time as illusionism for the general public. The proof of this success is the long remembered disbelief in the final image of Marlene Dietrich setting out into the desert sands on spike heels in search of Gary Cooper. C. A. Lejeune of *The London Observer* has described this finale as one of the most absurd of all time. Yet to single out any one detail of a film for disbelief is to believe in the rest, and to believe in MOROCCO's California desert is to believe in Sternberg's dream décor. What Sternberg and many of his more gifted Hollywood and UFA studio colleagues proved is that consistency of style is ultimately more convincing than documentary certification. Sternberg, in particu-

lar, creates conviction by motivating his milieu with light and shadow. In a world of illusions, his camera suggests, everything is possible and nothing is necessary. Poetry transcends plausibility when characters are too vividly depicted for common sense criteria of behavior. Again Sternberg prepares the way for his delirious dénouement with intimations of irrationality and perversity. When Dietrich materializes in top hat, white tie, and tails and is thereafter immortalized as the purveyor of pansexuality, the immediacy of impact makes Sternberg's gesture seem more gratuitous than it is. Aside from the lilting vertiginousness of vice involved in Marlene's mock seduction of a flustered female, Sternberg achieves all sorts of economies of expression in Marlene's meaningful masquerade. Her costume, for example, mocks Menjou's. Here is a representation of the civilized European male as seen from the point of view of the woman he seeks to seduce with infinite patience, but yet the effect is not one of pure parody. Neither Sternberg nor Dietrich is completely sure of all the psychological twists. There is always chance, romance, and the inspiration of improvisation. Dietrich fondles the hair of the girl she is going to outrage with a kiss, but she has none of the complacent confidence Garbo displays in a similar situation in QUEEN CHRISTINA. Dietrich's impersonation is an adventure, an act of bravado that subtly alters her conception of herself as a woman, and what begins as self-expression ends as self-sacrifice, perhaps the path also of Sternberg as an artist.

When Dietrich asks Cooper if he wants to buy her apples, this obvious double entendre is rescued from crudity by the genuine awkwardness and uncertainty of the two players. Dietrich here is in the process of discovering herself, and the awakening of self-awareness visibly delights her. Never again will she be so defenselessly charming, so personally accessible to the audience at each instant of her performance. As for Cooper, it is difficult to believe that this natural American landmark ever planted a rose behind his ear or flourished a fan behind which he stole a discreet kiss from Dietrich. That Sternberg brings off such uncharacteristic affectations by Cooper is a mark of the director's fluency in the language of gesture.

In a limited sense, MOROCCO is a reversal of THE BLUE ANGEL in that a woman is humbled by a man. As in THE BLUE ANGEL, however, there is genuine interplay

Preparing the long tracking shot in MOROCCO (1930)

is peculiarly modern. Sternberg did not always succeed in reconciling style with feeling, but he does with Menjou's La Bessière, part stoic, part sybarite, part satanist. Audiences sometimes laugh at him as a well-mannered masochist, particularly in the dinner scene of Dietrich's renunciation, but Sternberg has never been as close to any character as he is to this elegant expatriate who tries to maintain the decorum of his public posture as he watches the one great obsession of an otherwise ordered life disappear forever into the desert. In Menjou's pained politeness of expression is engraved the age-old tension between the Apollonian and Dionysian demands of art, between pride in restraint and passion in excess, between the formal protocol of self-control and the spontaneous eruptions of self-gratification. In the midst of his fears about Dietrich's decision, Menjou apologizes for not having listened to the babbling of a French general (played by Sternberg's old mentor, Emile Chautard). When Dietrich kisses him goodbye, Menjou clutches her wrist in one last spasmodic reflex of passion, but the other hand retains its poise at his side, the gestures of form and feeling thus conflicting to the very end of the drama. If Sternberg had been nothing more than a delirious decorator, his art would have long since faded into the limbo of fashion, but, like Menjou, Sternberg never loses his composure, and, consequently, he never sacrifices the contemplative aspect of his compositions for easy effects of parody and pathos.

between male and female, but even more, there is a perverse interchange of masculine and feminine characteristics. If Gary Cooper's Tom Brown is Sternberg's most narcissistic hero, Marlene Dietrich is the supreme lover, male or female, and hers is the most romantic gesture in Sternberg's visual vocabulary. The complaint that a woman in high heels would not walk off into the desert is nonetheless meaningless. A dream does not require endurance, only the will to act.

When the Pasha of Marrakesh insisted to Sternberg that MOROCCO must have been shot on location, the director replied with ironic modesty that any confusion of illusion and reality "was no more than an accidental resemblance, a flaw due to my lack of talent to avoid such similarity." The real Morocco would, of course, have crushed Sternberg, Dietrich, Cooper, and Menjou under the weight of extraneous details. To make the plot fit the clime, expressiveness would have been sacrificed to the needless exposition of establishing shots. MOROCCO is the product of a period when movies could still create their own mystique, and if Sternberg's sets look less real today, his characters ring even more true. There is a delicacy of regret in Menjou's stylish suffering at the hands of Dietrich that

1931 DISHONORED (Paramount) Directed by Josef von Sternberg. Script by Daniel N. Rubin based on a story by Josef von Sternberg. Photographed by Lee Garmes. Sets by Hans Dreier. With Marlene Dietrich (X 27), Victor McLaglen (Lieutenant Kranau), Lew Cody (Colonel Kovrin), Gustav von Seyffertitz (Secret Service Head), Warner Oland (General Von Hindau), Barry Norton (Young Lieutenant), Davison Clark (Court Officer), and Wilfred Lucas (General Dymov).

"The company decided to title the film DISHONORED," Sternberg recalls in his autobiography, "disregarding my protest that the lady spy was not dishonored but killed by a firing squad." In its time, the spy genre to which DISHONORED belongs was taken even less seriously than soap opera. Based on a Sternberg story called "X 27," the film suffers from its episodic structure. Victor McLaglen, a fugitive from the John Ford galaxy, was so far from being the ideal Sternbergian hero that Marlene Dietrich was unable to strike the sparks of her previous encounters with Hans Albers in THE BLUE ANGEL and Gary Cooper in MOROCCO. In Sternberg's conception of direction as total creation, the control of casting is essential to the expression of the director's idea, but such control has seldom been granted to any Hollywood director. In fact, the exigencies of production schedules everywhere in the world impose certain casting limitations on the most personal and most individual of directors and Sternberg's predilection for reducing performers to mere details of the décor hardly endeared him to all the players he might have wanted to use at one time or another.

Despite or perhaps because of its thematic slightness, DISHONORED is Sternberg's funniest film. The grave deliberateness and delicate grace with which Dietrich plies her trade as a prostitute gives the show away from the very beginning. In no other film does Dietrich so self-consciously try on different roles for size and style. Her fantasy prostitute is no less committed than her fake peasant to the service of a love which transcends the trivial issues of politics. If Dietrich lives for love in THE BLUE ANGEL, and sacrifices for love in MOROCCO, she dies for love in DISHONORED.

"Let me die," she asks, "in the uniform in which I served, not my country, but my countrymen." Let her die, Sternberg implies, for being faithful to her nature as a woman, for matters of sex rather than state. When an idealistic young officer refuses to participate in the execution, Sternberg quickly cuts away from the

MOROCCO (1930). Adolphe Menjou and Marlene Dietrich. Courtesy Herman Weinberg

youth's foolish forensics to Dietrich's affirmative application of her last earthly makeup. This inspired injection of the cosmetic into the cosmic makes the audience laugh at the absurdity of female vanity, and there *is* humor in a situation balanced so precariously between gallantry and ghoulishness. It would have been a cheap joke for almost any other director, but for Sternberg it is closer to being an article of faith. The director's equation of sexual magnetism with political power is more explicit later in THE SCARLET EMPRESS, but it is never the sheer utilitarianism of sex with which Sternberg is concerned in his political parables. One might compare in this context Garbo's relatively routine spy-vamp character in MATA HARI with Dietrich's delicious dedication to experiences beyond the technical limits of espionage.

For Sternberg, sex is less the hard currency of politics than its shaping spirit. His political males strut about in their ridiculous costumes, genuflect before idiotic deities of war and country, conduct intrigues on a childish level of deception, and then pass judgment on the only life-giving force in their midst. Yet it is Dietrich who ultimately passes judgment on her judges by choosing to die as a woman without a cause in a picture without a moral. There may be also in the final spectacle of Dietrich's death more than a trace of directorial fantasy and wish fulfillment. To transpose Wilde while mangling his meter, each director kills the thing he loves, the coward does it with a fade, the brave man with a cut!

1931 AN AMERICAN TRAGEDY

(Paramount) Directed by Josef von Sternberg. Script by Samuel Hoffenstein based on the novel by Theodore Dreiser (adapted by von Sternberg and Samuel Hoffenstein). Photographed by Lee Garmes. Sets by Hans Dreier. With Phillips Holmes (Clyde Griffiths), Sylvia Sidney (Roberta Alden), Frances Dee (Sondra Finchley), Irving Pichel (Orville Mason), Frederick Burton (Samuel Griffiths), Claire McDowell (Mrs. Samuel Griffiths), Wallace Middleton (Gilbert Griffiths), Vivian Winston (Myra Griffiths), Emmett Corrigan (Belknap), Lucille La Verne (Mrs. Asa Griffiths), Charles B. Middleton (Jephson), Albert Hart (Titus Alden), Fanny Midgely (Mrs. Alden),

DISHONORED (1931). Marlene Dietrich and Victor McLaglen

Arline Judge (Bella Griffiths), Evelyn Pierce (Bertine Cranston), Arnold Korff (Judge), Elizabeth Forrester (Jill Trumbell), Russell Powell (Coroner Fred Heit), Imboden Parrish (Earl Newcomb), and Richard Kramer (Deputy Sheriff Kraut).

AN AMERICAN TRAGEDY was in its time a contretemps of classic proportions. The internationally acclaimed Russian director Sergei Eisenstein had been invited by Paramount to transfer the Theodore Dreiser novel to the screen, but the treatment he prepared was rejected. Sternberg was asked to make the film instead, and Dreiser, who greatly admired Eisenstein's script, protested. After the film was completed, Dreiser sued Paramount to stop its exhibition, and lost his case.

Sternberg's own recollections of this episode in his career are consistent with what finally materialized on the screen. "When, two years or so after we first met, Eisenstein came to Hollywood to undertake the task of making Dreiser's novel, I welcomed him and the two capable assistants he brought with him. I talked with all three quite often. I never discussed Eisenstein's assignments with him. I had troubles of my own, and if my memory serves me correctly, I left for Europe before he had started the manuscript on which he planned to base his film. When I returned he was gone, and I was told that the scenario submitted to the studio heads had been too long and incomprehensible for them. This failed to arouse any wonder in me. My own scenarios had always been incomprehensible to the dozen or so overlords who considered themselves competent to translate words into pictures, but because my films were successful with the masses, and, what was thought to be more important, created 'stellar values,' they for a while allowed me to write scenarios that were Greek to them. I never saw Eisenstein's script and, for that matter, I never heard from him again, except indirectly once or twice. He had gone to Mexico to make a film, which I think was sponsored by Upton Sinclair, and encountered trouble there also, and finally returned to Russia. While waiting for my next assignment, after a trip to the West Indies, I was approached by Adolph Zukor. He told me that the company had a dormant investment of half a million dollars in AN AMERICAN TRAGEDY, and pleaded with me to undertake to salvage this by making an inexpensive version of it. Having read the book years ago, I agreed, and went to work writing my own script. I eliminated the sociological elements, which, in my opinion, were far from being responsible for the dramatic accident with which Dreiser had concerned himself."

Under this creative cloud AN AMERICAN TRAGEDY has been reviewed less for the film it was than for the film it should have been. Where Eisenstein proposed a deterministic treatment of the subject to absolve Clyde of the crime committed in the name of a materialistic society, Sternberg preferred to consider Clyde guilty of an act conditioned by the furtive prurience of his environment. To equate the difference between Eisenstein and Sternberg with the difference between Marx and Freud would be an oversimplification, but the thirties were an epoch when desire ran a poor second to dialectics in serious discussions of the cinema.

Curiously, Sylvia Sidney's poor girl is more sympathetic here than Frances Dee's rich girl, whereas in the 1951 George Stevens version (A PLACE IN THE SUN), Elizabeth Taylor's rich girl is more sympathetic than Shelley Winters' poor girl. Sternberg thus turns his audience against his hero while Stevens is enlisting sympathy for his, a distinction further emphasized by the lyrical American Dream close-ups of Stevens as opposed to the chillingly objective middle distance shots of Sternberg. Sternberg was actually more faithful to Dreiser than was Stevens, but by 1951 fidelity to novels was no longer as much a canon of faith as it had been in 1931.

The one key scene in the film takes place in the factory where Phillips Holmes arranges the seduction of

AN AMERICAN TRAGEDY (1931). Phillips Holmes and Sylvia Sidney, below left, and below right, Phillips Holmes

Sidney. He has forced her to capitulate by threatening never to see her again. She hands him a note when he passes by the assembly line where she is working. Holmes furtively opens the note in a secluded spot where his expression cannot be seen by the factory girls, and a smile of triumph flickers across his normally phlegmatic features. Since he is seen at an objective distance, he is irrevocably guilty at that very moment for his sexual presumption. Sternberg's sympathy for Sidney is expressed mainly through his coolness to Holmes, and the virtuous aspect of the director's personality is reaffirmed.

The recurring water images serve as stylistic determinants of the hero's destiny, and, as a side effect, the temperature of the characterization remains cool. Nonetheless Holmes slowly, almost imperceptibly releases his repressed feelings at the very moment he is no longer free to make moral decisions. This liberation is expressed by nothing more than the flickering smile which creases his features as he accepts for the first time his mother's love and concern. What must have moved Sternberg always in AN AMERICAN TRAGEDY was the high price Clyde had to pay for self-knowledge. In this respect, at least, Sternberg removes Clyde from under Dreiser's materialistic microscope and endows him with autonomous feelings with which Sternberg himself can identify.

SHANGHAI EXPRESS (1932). Clive Brook, Marlene Dietrich

Sternberg's lack of concern for Dreiser's "sociological elements" extends to the machinery in the factory which employs Dreiser's protagonists. Sternberg sees the machinery simply as the force of fate in motion much as he saw the dredge in THE SALVATION HUNTERS as the representation of cosmic futility. The director is impressed by the inexorability of mechanical motion as a metaphor for the inexorable lapsing of life. The fact that machinery is also changing the tempo and texture of existence never seems to be expressible in Sternberg's style. He seems oblivious to the claims and clamors of Progress and Dynamic Modernism. AN AMERICAN TRAGEDY, like most of his other films, remains focused on the dilemmas of desire which torment men and women eternally.

1932 SHANGHAI EXPRESS (Paramount) Directed by Josef von Sternberg. Script by Jules Furthman based on a story by Harry Hervey. Photographed by Lee Garmes. Sets by Hans Dreier. Gowns by Travis Banton. With Marlene Dietrich (Shanghai Lily), Clive Brook (Captain Donald Harvey), Anna May Wong (Hui Fei), Warner Oland (Henry Chang), Eugene Palette (Sam Salt), Lawrence Grant (Mr. Carmichael), Louise Closser Hale (Mrs. Haggerty), Gustav von Seyffertitz (Eric Baum), and Emile Chautard (Major Lenard).

Sternberg's flair for impulsive fatalism finds more play in SHANGHAI EXPRESS than elsewhere. A veritable GRAND HOTEL on rails, the steam-puffing vehicle from Peking to Shanghai conveys Anna May Wong and Warner Oland toward a fateful rendezvous with dishonor and death. Eugene Pallette, Lawrence Grant and Louise Closser Hale offer a pinch of Anglo-Saxon pragmatism with which the audience can identify in Sternberg's otherwise disoriented Orient, and Gustav von Seyffertitz and Emile Chautard donate a distinctively Sternbergian tone to the proceedings, Seyffertitz as a smuggler making a disreputable departure from the moral stability of his roles in THE DOCKS OF NEW YORK and DISHONORED, and Emile Chautard as Major Lenard reflecting once more Sternberg's gratitude to his mentor of less than a decade before.

Marlene Dietrich and Clive Brook carry the heart of the drama, and a beating heart it is despite all the gloss of intrigue and illusion. SHANGHAI EXPRESS marks the fourth and last full-scale collaboration between Sternberg and the legendary Lee Garmes, and certainly even in Sternberg's cinema it is difficult to find any more lushly photographed films than MOROCCO, AN AMERICAN TRAGEDY, DISHONORED, and SHANGHAI EXPRESS. (Sternberg and Garmes were later involved tangentially together in the wild Vidor-Selznick-Busch western, DUEL IN THE SUN.) The delirious visualization of SHANGHAI EXPRESS has suggested dramatic vacuity to a hostile critic like John Grierson, and even a pro-Sternberg reviewer like Robert E. Sherwood dismissed the dramatic content of what he considered otherwise a stunning spectacle.

This is the movie in which Marlene Dietrich tells Clive Brook: "It took more than one man to change my name to Shanghai Lily." Brook reacts to this news with a degree of stoic calm befitting a Noel Coward character of that era, and it becomes difficult for most audiences to take the Dietrich-Brook relationship very seriously from that moment on. Yet Brook's performance is deeply felt despite the stylization of Sternberg's direction of dialogue, and the last ten minutes of the film are as emotionally profound as anything Sternberg has ever attempted. Brook's ritualistic delivery of dialogue, jumped time and again two sentences in one breath, serves as a vocal mask for the pride and passion which seethe beneath the controlled surface. Once the issues of the melodrama have been resolved, he waits for Dietrich to make some gesture of explanation or expiation. She makes none. Her face merely taunts him in a myriad of mirrors until he surrenders to the illusion she represents, but on her terms rather than his. At first glance, this seems like the conventional happy ending, but it is as bitterly ironic as Lubitsch's ANGEL where Herbert Marshall is forced to accept Dietrich in terms of the Pirandellian masquerade she has devised to deceive him. Yet where the Lubitschean moment of capitulation is overlaid with comedy, the equivalent Sternbergian moment is painfully unadorned. That love can be unconditional is a hard truth for American audiences to accept at any time. Depression audiences found it especially difficult to appreciate Sternberg's Empire of Desire ruled by Marlene Dietrich. If, in fact, SHANGHAI EXPRESS was successful at all, it was because it was completely misunderstood as a mindless adventure.

It is remarkable that Sternberg managed to stylize performances as late into the talkies as he did. Standard aesthetic doctrine of the Anglo-Russian school stipulated that silent films were a director's medium and sound films were an actor's medium. The argument behind this doctrine was that silent directors, or at least some directors, could create performances in the cutting room à la Kuleshov-Mozhukin, but that dialogue created its own rhythms which were determined more by actors than by directors. The weakness of this argument in practice was that only the most obvious acting effects could be created through montage. Chaplin, the greatest screen actor, silent or sound, created his performances mainly through an integral frame with a bare minimum of intercut reaction shots. The subtler silent actors like Conrad Veidt, Richard Barthelmess, Adolphe Menjou, and Ronald Colman functioned best by underplaying the reactions their director's montage prescribed for them. Once the talkies had arrived, cross-cutting for its own sake became a foolish function of Hollywood star cinema. Sternberg's camera style generally eschewed pointless cutting within scenes, and thus anticipated a modern non-montage director like Antonioni.

1932 BLONDE VENUS (Paramount)

Directed by Josef von Sternberg. Script by Jules Furthman and S. K. Lauren based on a story by Josef von Sternberg. Photographed by Bert Glennon. Sets by Wiard Ihnen. Songs: "Hot Voodoo" and "You Little So and So" by Sam Coslow and Ralph Rainger; "I Couldn't Be Annoyed" by Leo Robin and Dick Whiting. With Marlene Dietrich (Helen Faraday), Herbert Marshall (Edward Faraday), Cary Grant (Nick Townsend), Dickie Moore (Johnny Faraday), Gene Morgan (Ben Smith), Rita La Roy ("Taxi Belle" Hooper), Robert Emmett O'Connor (Dan O'Connor), Sidney Toler (Detective Wilson), and Cecil Cunningham (Nightclub Hostess).

The plot of BLONDE VENUS exploits the sordid self-sacrifice which movies of this era prescribed for its female stars. Greta Garbo, Margaret Sullavan, Tallulah Bankhead, Bette Davis, Constance Bennett, Barbara Stanwyck, and Ginger Rogers paraded down Sin Street, usually more sinned against than sinning, for the sake of home and hearth. BLONDE VENUS could not have been produced after the censors clamped down in 1934, however, and thus quite accidentally a picaresque potboiler of its time has acquired a distinctive period flavor. The picture starts off slowly with an idyllic courtship of Marlene Dietrich by Herbert Marshall, who rather abruptly burdens her with a son, the dimpled Dickie Moore, whom Marlene is called upon to mother solicitously. Dietrich clearly lacks Garbo's sweeter registers of innocence and maternal warmth. Garbo can gravitate between Freddy Bartholomew and Fredric March in ANNA KARENINA without sacrificing the emotional cohesion of her characterization, but Dietrich becomes unconvincing whenever she is called upon to express emotional directness. Dietrich's irrepressible irony and speculative humor make her a dubious hausfrau indeed, and consequently BLONDE VENUS stumbles along until Dietrich begins dragging her child around Sternberg's Skid Row America from assignation to assignation. Sternberg's style muffles the sordidness here as it has muffled the violence in his gangster films. Dietrich's descent is less odious than Orphic, and her rise is completely redeeming.

Dietrich dominates the action throughout to a degree that reduces dramatic tension. Herbert Marshall, as the long-suffering husband for whose health Marlene becomes a gangster's mistress, is a polite masochist with none of the persistent passion which motivates Sternberg's most striking heroes. (Marshall is at his best under Lubitsch in TROUBLE IN PARADISE and ANGEL where he fittingly floats through the action in a semi-detached daze.) The gangster is played by a still callow Cary Grant, whose pairing with Dietrich is not very memorable. Yet it is doubtful that Grant and Dietrich would ever have worked as a satisfactory team. For all its smooth grace, Grant's style is essentially realistic. He is a real person, not next door necessarily, but somewhere. Dietrich is a fantasy figure from nowhere, and no actress can play properly with Grant without some sort of address. By the same token, Grant would only intrude on Dietrich's style of perpetual mystery with the demystifying lurch of his probing personality. That is why Grant is so superbly cast in Hitchcock's films: he supplies the proper note of reality Hitchcock requires to orchestrate his suspense. Historians of film technology can note one of the period's worst process shots in a sequence where Dietrich and Grant stare soulfully at the camera while allegedly riding the surf in a speedboat. Technically as well as spiritually, Sternberg's heart didn't seem to be in that bogus outdoors scene.

Yet if BLONDE VENUS is essentially a one-woman show, it is still one of the best examples of the genre for its time. Greta Garbo's equivalent SUSAN LENNOX— HER FALL AND RISE was virtually a disaster. Garbo remains interesting of course even under Robert Z. Leonard's uninspired direction, but around her there is nothing except chaos and mediocrity. By contrast, Sternberg's style begins gripping its hackneyed material halfway through the movie, and by the end his star has managed to move the audience with an uncompromising affirmation of her fearless femaleness, an affirmation comparable in spirit if not in scale with the ultimate affirmation of THE BLUE ANGEL. Curiously, the fact that the plot of BLONDE VENUS lacks surface conviction gives it a certain freedom in its fantasizing, and not the least of its charms is its careless regard of Dietrich the Woman trying to cope with the demands of her myth. That her nightclub numbers are utterly unmotivated in terms of the plot is a key to the extreme stylization of Dietrich's character, extreme, that is, even for Sternberg.

The pre-credit scene of THE LOVE GODDESSES, a film compilation of screen sirens, shows Marlene emerging from her monkey suit in the voodoo number of BLONDE VENUS. The conception of beauty as the beast is stirring, but the song that accompanies the conception is unfortunately forgettable. Between "Falling in Love Again" in THE BLUE ANGEL and her rendezvous with Rimski-Korsakov in THE DEVIL IS A WOMAN, Dietrich was not well-served by the music on the sound-track, and there was nothing that even Sternberg could do to transform such tunesmiths as Leo Robin, Karl Hajos, Sam Coslow, Ralph Rainger, Dick Whiting, and Andrea Setaro into George Gershwin, Jerome Kern, Cole Porter, Richard Rodgers, Harold Arlen, and Irving Berlin. Direction, after all, is one thing, and alchemy quite another.

There are interesting incongruities in some of the peripheral characterizations, particularly a delicious moment of anti-typecasting irony when the middle-aged Lesbian-like Cecil Cunningham clucks sympathetically to Dietrich that she (Cecil) has a kid of her own, and

knows what it is to be on the run. This is the wearily jaded side of Sternberg, a side far too wearily jaded even to smile at its own conceits.

Another side of Sternberg is reflected in the curiously ambiguous characterization of Sidney Toler's Detective Wilson, who enters knowingly as the cryptic player of a cat-and-mouse game with Dietrich, but who unexpectedly turns out to be an ordinary bloke genuinely attracted by her allure. What is odd about this development is that the character makes little sense unless he knows as much as he suggests. Audiences tend to be impressed by characters who are a few steps ahead of the plot, and it takes a great deal of directorial restraint to keep actors from pretending to know more than there is in the script. If anything, Sternberg's characters are generally a bit slower than the audience. It may take a whole film or a whole lifetime for a Sternbergian character to find out the truth about himself and one or two other people, and then that truth may be savored for only a moment or an hour before death, disaster, or disgrace. For Sternberg the truth is worth knowing whatever the price because there is dramatic beauty in the process of self-awakening. As for Dietrich's fall and rise in BLONDE VENUS, Sternberg's point is that what Marlene lacks in character she more than makes up in style, and genuine style can never be dragged through the dirt indefinitely.

1934 THE SCARLET EMPRESS (Paramount)

Directed by Josef von Sternberg. Script by Manuel Komroff from a diary of Catherine the Great. Photographed by Bert Glennon. Sets by Hans Dreier, Peter Ballbusch, and Richard Kollorsz. Titles and effects by Gordon Jennings. Costumes by Travis Banton. Musical score based on Tschaikowsky and Mendelssohn arranged by John M. Leopold and W. Frank Harling. With Marlene Dietrich (Sophia Frederica, later Catherine II), John Lodge (Count Alexei), Sam Jaffe (Grand Duke Peter), Louise Dresser (Empress Elizabeth), Maria Sieber (Catherine as a child), C. Aubrey Smith (Prince

August), Ruthelma Stevens (Countess Elizabeth), Olive Tell (Princess Johanna), Gavin Gordon (Gregory Orloff), Jameson Thomas (Lieutenant Ovtsyn), Hans von Twardowski (Ivan Shuvolov), Davison Clark (Archimandrite Simeon Tevedovsky), and Jane Darwell, Erville Alderson, Marie Wells, Harry Woods, Edward Van Sloan, Phillip Sleeman, John Davidson, Gerald Fielding, James Burke, Belle Stoddard Johnstone, Nadine Beresford, Eunice Moore, Petra McAllister, Blanche Rose, James Marcus, Thomas C. Blythe, Clyde David, Richard Alexander, Hal Boyer, Barbara Sabichi, and Dima Smirnova.

THE SCARLET EMPRESS is Sternberg's most sumptuous exercise in style, a tapestry of tyranny so intricately woven and so luminously lit that audiences and critics of the time were stupefied. The big sleeper of 1934 was Frank Capra's IT HAPPENED ONE NIGHT which titillated Depression audiences with the democratic spectacle of a virile reporter knocking the nonsense out of a hoity-toity society dame. Audiences were thus hardly in the mood to be exhilarated by the ecstatic

triumph of Marlene Dietrich's sensuality over the infantile cruelties of Old Russia. Even Paul Czinner's relatively conventional CATHERINE THE GREAT of that same year with that Viennese virtuoso Elizabeth Bergner was more favorably received. Bergner's interpretation of Catherine was relentlessly sympathetic as with stagey self-indulgence she searched her mirror for true love while her followers were destroying the forces of her mad husband. Bergner was in that fluttery, fussy Viennese tradition which has featured Luise Rainer, Maria Schell, and, most gloriously of all, Lilli Palmer. Back in 1934, however, Elizabeth Bergner's status as a stage performer made her automatically superior to a purely cinematic creation like Marlene Dietrich. (Even Bergner's revolting Rosalind in AS YOU LIKE IT gave her an edge over a mere movie star who had never tackled Shakespeare.) Also, Czinner's matter-of-fact direction and pacing seemed more in the mode than Sternberg's elaborate compositions and discursive camera movements. When Czinner had Bergner run down marble stairs, he fostered a feeling of spacious emptiness so that Bergner could be emphasized even in long-shot, whereas all of Dietrich's descents are drenched in Sternberg's meaningful décor.

Sternberg's conception of Catherine is far more audacious in all aspects than Czinner's. Where Bergner's Prince is a moderately mad Douglas Fairbanks, Jr. who seems to be suffering from migraine headaches, Marlene's mate is a pop-eyed Sam Jaffe whose insanity never lacks for objective and visual correlatives. Jaffe's hi-jinks with a voyeur's brace and bit and a horde of pet Hessians struck some critics as antics more appropriate for Harpo Marx than Russian royalty, and this is more a compliment to Jaffe's performance than these critics realized. THE SCARLET EMPRESS shatters the decorum which was spreading over the American cinema like a shroud. Its very outrageousness is an index of the repressive reasonableness of most movie-making of its time, and nothing is more outrageous than Sternberg's decision to be clear rather than coy about the sexual politics of Catherine the Great.

Nonetheless Dietrich is not entirely effective in the opening sequences in which she impersonates an innocent but impulsive German girl. As Marlene lacked maternal warmth in BLONDE VENUS, she lacks maidenly modesty in THE SCARLET EMPRESS. Her subsequent metamorphosis into the mistress of a male realm thus seems mechanically contrived because the iconography of what she is transcends the drama of what she becomes. We see Catherine the Great through Marlene Dietrich less than Marlene Dietrich through Catherine the Great, and there can be no drama of self-awakening in a personality that provides all the answers before any questions are asked. The sweet curiosity of MOROCCO has now hardened into glacial guile. Romantic adventures have degenerated into erotic escapades; warm passion has frozen into calculating carnality.

The Sternberg-Dietrich collaboration has now entered the phase of allegory over irony, and both THE SCARLET EMPRESS and THE DEVIL IS A WOMAN will always seem more fascinating to the Sternberg-Dietrich specialists than to general audiences. For one thing, Sternberg seems to have been driven, perhaps partly by the censors, to retreat into the exotic past. Up to now, Sternberg has confined himself for the most part to a world encompassed within his own lifetime, and there is something to be said for an artist who imposes his personal vision on the present. Though Sternberg continues to comment on the present in THE SCARLET EMPRESS, his meaning is somewhat obscured by the massive detail of period recreation.

Clarence Brown has acknowledged that the table-tracking orgy opening of ANNA KARENINA was inspired by Sternberg's banquet bouleversements in THE SCARLET EMPRESS, but a comparison of the two films reveals the difference between routine eclecticism and relentless expressiveness. For Sternberg a table is not merely a table, but a battlefield around which powerful personalities are arrayed, fully armed with metaphorical knives and forks. The continuous visual field provided by his crane enables him to trace the course of the battle with the steady subtlety which would have been denied to him by mere cross-cutting. Dietrich and Jaffe are more evenly matched than one would expect, and Louise Dresser as the Czarina and John Lodge as the sardonic substitute for the impotent Jaffe fit with curious authoritativeness into the baroque background. Lodge, later Governor of Connecticut and Ambassador to

Spain, never had much of a film career, but even his stiff handsomeness seems to fall into place in THE SCARLET EMPRESS where stylish virility is sufficient stimulus for Marlene's mocking eyes.

What probably disturbed Marxist critics of the thirties even more than Sternberg's ruthless eroticism was a detached view of power as an orgiastic experience. The murder of Jaffe is viewed as an ambiguous act, and Sternberg does not shrink from the pity even a grotesque tyrant evokes at the moment of his downfall. Jaffe dies as he has lived, loathing Dietrich with the last breath in his body. Contrast this with Fairbanks dying in Czinner's CATHERINE with his love for Catherine still intact. The fact that Dietrich has aligned herself with the Church and the Army against Jaffe would hardly make her more sympathetic to modern liberals, and her donation of her diamonds to the poor seems like an ingeniously dramatic method of displaying them. Sternberg and Dietrich cannot suppress an irrepressible irreverence toward this gesture of paternalism toward the peasants. For the most part, THE SCARLET EMPRESS plays most humorously as a parody of good intentions in politics through the symbols of sexual sublimation. It is almost outrageously simple to understand the significance of Jaffe's saber thrust at Dietrich's throat, a thrust she mockingly parries with a wisp of chiffon which sheathes the saber. In the Sternbergian State the bedroom and the throne room are one and the same, and no conversion table is required to convert sexual power into political power. Dietrich's rapturous ride up the palace steps at the head of her Imperial Cavalry is the visual correlative of soaring sexual ecstasy, and land reform would seem to be the last thing on her mind when she finally turns to confront her subjects with the glittering eyes of now utterly unrestrained sensuality. The tyranny of a subhuman superego has been replaced by the tyranny of a superhuman libido. The dimensions of Sternberg's kingdom of the senses are deliriously defined for the first and last time, but Depression audiences couldn't have cared less.

1935 THE DEVIL IS A WOMAN

(Paramount) Directed by Josef von Sternberg. Script by John Dos Passos and Sam Winston based on the novel "The Woman and the Puppet" by Pierre Louys. Music by Rimski-Korsakov ("Caprice Espagnol"), Ralph Rainger, and Andrea Setaro, Song: "Three Sweethearts Have I" by Leo Robin and Ralph Rainger. Photographed by Sternberg and Lucien Ballard. Sets by Hans Dreier. Costumes by Travis Banton. With Marlene Dietrich (Concha Perez), Lionel Atwill (Don Pasqual), Cesar Romero (Antonio Galvan), Edward Everett Horton (Don Paquito), Alison Skipworth (Senora Perez), Don Alvarado (Morenito), Morgan Wallace (Dr. Mendez), Tempe Pigott (Tuerta), Jil Dennett (Maria), Lawrence Grant (Conductor), Charles Sellon (Letter Writer), Luisa Espinal (Gypsy Dancer), Hank Mann (Foreman, Snowbound Train), Edwin Maxwell (Superintendent, Tobacco Factory), Donald Reed, and Eddie Borden.

THE DEVIL IS A WOMAN is the last of the Sternberg-Dietrich sagas, and never before has Sternberg seemed as visible as he does here in the saturnine silhouette of Lionel Atwill, the morose victim of frustration and folly. There is something decidedly downbeat in Dietrich's being flanked by Atwill and Cesar Romero at this stage of her career, and the film's reputation for campiness can be attributed largely to this secondary

THE SCARLET EMPRESS (1934). Sam Jaffe. Courtesy George Eastman House

casting. Atwill has been too frequently identified with the mad scientist (from Atwill to Zucco) repertory, while Romero has been considered a lightweight personality throughout his career though it is hard to see how Joel McCrea, for whom Romero was a last-minute replacement, would have been much of an improvement. Yet if Atwill and Romero do not attain the high level of Brook, Bancroft, Jannings, Menjou, and Cooper, they are far from being inadequate for Sternberg's ironies. They play fools, but not foolishly. They are the last lovers Sternberg has postulated for Dietrich's screen incarnation, and their apparent absurdity only marks the death of desire.

The lack of overt sexual commitment on the part of Dietrich's "Concha" may be attributed to the intentional sadism of the Pierre Louys character or the intransigence of the Hays Office or both. Sternberg's original title, CAPRICE ESPAGNOL, may have originally seemed more relevant to the final film than THE DEVIL IS A WOMAN, but there is no gainsaying Dietrich's devilishness, particularly when she tells one of her admirers, "If you really loved me, you would have killed yourself."

As Sternberg recalls the title alteration and the attendant atmosphere: "My last and most unpopular film of this series was based on a book by Pierre Louys; John Dos Passos, in bed with undulant fever, was trying to help in writing the adaptation. With the dice loaded so that I could not win, I paid a final tribute to the lady I had seen lean against the wings of a Berlin stage, at the same time planning an affectionate salute to Spain and its traditions. As if I were a computing machine, I built scene after scene to form an exact pattern, allowing nothing but the future audience to escape my attention, and adding to my normal duties the task of handling the camera mechanism. The intention was to call the film CAPRICCIO ESPAGNOL (sic). This was negated by Mr. Lubitsch, in full charge of the studio, and though he was unable to interfere with my production, he set his seal on it by altering the title to THE DEVIL IS A WOMAN. This accent is not mine. Though Mr. Lubitsch's poetic intention to suggest altering the sex of the devil was meant to aid in selling the picture, it did not do so.

"The film was banned by the Spanish government, which, in turn, was banned by Generalissimo Franco, but not before its diplomats made protestations to our government that caused the work to be withdrawn from circulation. The ostensible reason given was that the Guardia Civil had been shown to be ineffectual in curbing a riotous carnival during which the action of the film takes place. The film, shown only at The Museum of Modern Art in New York until it was shipped to Venice in 1959 for its film festival, was again put into limited circulation in 1961."

Sternberg's "riotous carnival" is in the great transfigured tinsel tradition of UNDERWORLD, THE DRAG NET, THE DOCKS OF NEW YORK, and DISHONORED. It is amazing how little space Sternberg requires to evoke an empire, and how little time to evoke an era. The sheer economy of the director's mise-en-scène has seldom been appreciated largely because he has been artful enough to make it seem opulent. In this respect, Sternberg and Stroheim are related to each other stylistically in the way Rommel and Montgomery were related to each other tactically in North Africa during the Second World War. Where Rommel would disguise his trucks as tanks to look stronger, Montgomery would disguise his tanks as trucks to look weaker. For all his vaunted opulence, Stroheim looks shoddy next to Sternberg because of a lack of imagination in deploying his visual forces. Stroheim was simply too literal to understand that the appearances of things were more impressive than the things themselves. Sternberg conversely understood the essence of enchantment as the power of selective rather than exhaustive detail.

Nonetheless, THE DEVIL IS A WOMAN is far more than a decorator's delight. The dramatic resolution of its characters is complete despite a tedious red herring narration by Atwill. There is something deliciously funny about the Sternberg variation on the familiar plot device of the older and wiser man warning the younger and wilder about the dire designs of a *femme fatale* Inevitably there is the misunderstanding: the younger man thinks the older man is motivated by his own lecherous designs, and the older man sighs wearily about such unfounded suspicions. Here Sternberg pulls the switch: Atwill *is* motivated by his own lecherous designs, and the whole narration is revealed as dishonest in its didactic intention.

Despite the sumptuousness of its surface, THE DEVIL IS A WOMAN is Sternberg's coldest film. Its art is bone dry; its feelings parched in a desert of despair. Even the film's silliness around the edges is measured precisely, and nothing is sillier than the occasional stabs at social consciousness, starting with a tobacco factory right out of *Carmen*. The humor of the film is derived less from the giddy comic relief of Edward Everett Horton's susceptible police captain than the wry amusement Lionel Atwill's "Don Pasqual" derives from his own suffering. The motif of the masks in the opening carnival sequence is carried through all of Dietrich's maddening deceptions, but Atwill persists in his passion because under the implied intelligence and urbanity of *his* mask lurk all the demons of desire. Every acquisitively cluttered, riotously disordered frame in which Atwill appears with Dietrich contributes to the inner rage and frustration of his apparently impassive characterization. This is how, ideally, Sternberg directs his players: not by tampering with their faces to provide self-explanatory grimaces, but by creating a visual context in which the most unobtrusive acting effects become eloquently expressive. Sternberg's décor is then not the meaningless background of the drama, but its very subject, peering through nets, veils, screens, shutters, bars, cages, mists, flowers, and fabrics to tantalize the male with fantasies of the female. Yet far from exaggerating his effects, Sternberg has perhaps calculated too closely. Dietrich, particularly, has been polished to an inhuman perfection beyond the accidental beauties of impulse and instinct. Her beauty is now so uninflected by dramatic development that even her cruelties are trivial.

Yet there was no denying that Dietrich was devastating. Cecelia Ager was particulary lucid on the subject in *Variety,* May 8, 1935: "Not even Garbo in the Orient has approached, for spectacular effects, Dietrich in Spain. With fringe, lace, sequins, carnations, chenille, nets, embroideries and shawls, Miss Dietrich is hung, wrapped, draped, swathed and festooned. Matching the sets in their profusion of arresting detail, her costumes are magnificent in the way they achieve a definite, clear-cut line despite their wealth of ornature, the way their knick-knacks fall into a pattern designed with flair and imagination solely to flatter and adore. Her costumes are completely incredible, but completely fascinating and suitable to THE DEVIL IS A WOMAN. They reek with glamour.

"Miss Dietrich's mask-like make-up and bizarre coiffures abound with beauty hints. When she lowers her shiny, heavy eyelids, it may be seen that artificial eyelashes are affixed only to the outer halves of her upper eyelids, intensifying thus the wide-spacing of her eyes and yielding them a provocative upward slant. Her lower lids are deliberately not accented with black, which would define the boundaries of her eyes and so limit their size. Her natural eyebrows have been blotted out and soaring new ones etched far above them, which, though they rob her eyes of anything other than a fixed, wondrous expression, assist the fantastic stylization that characterizes Miss Dietrich's pictorial treatment. Though her head is bedecked with an infinite variety of Spanish combs, flowers, shawls, fringes and veils, they've been arranged so as to frame her face, never to intrude their fripperies upon its expertly enhanced, submissive beauty. Miss Dietrich emerges in THE DEVIL IS A WOMAN as a glorious achievement, a supreme consolidation of the sartorial, make-up and photographic arts."

The question remains: why does Dietrich return to the mortally wounded Atwill at the end? Critics who believe in the unity of manner and meaning in Sternberg's work are struck by the fact that Dietrich is wearing black in the last scene. Black quite simply means death, and Marlene may be one of many deaths for both Atwill and Sternberg, the death of art, of poise, of poetry, of inspiration, of the will to continue. The Spanish setting with its inevitably fatalistic overtones may not have been entirely a capricious choice of locale. In what other country, past or present, real or imaginary, does dying demand more style than living? Sternberg did not know it at the time, but his sun was setting, and it has never really risen again. There are momentary spasms in CRIME AND PUNISHMENT, THE SHANGHAI GESTURE, and even CLAUDIUS, but for the rest, the divorce between manner and meaning is complete and incontestable until the final confessional of ANATAHAN. Still, as a goodbye to Dietrich, THE DEVIL IS A WOMAN is a more gallant gesture to one's once beloved than Orson Welles' murderous adieu to Rita Hayworth in THE LADY FROM SHANGHAI.

THE DEVIL IS A WOMAN (1935). Marlene Dietrich, center

1935 CRIME AND PUNISHMENT (Columbia)
Directed by Josef von Sternberg. Produced by
B. P. Schulberg. From the novel by Fyodor
Dostoevsky. Screenplay by S. K. Lauren and
Joseph Anthony. Photographed by Lucien Ballard.
Music by Louis Silvers. Sets by Stephen Goosens.
Costumes by Murray Mayer. Edited by Richard
Calhoon. With Edward Arnold (Inspector Porfiry),
Peter Lorre (Raskolnikov), Marian Marsh (Sonya),
Tala Birell (Antonya), Elizabeth Risdon
(Mrs. Raskolnikov), Robert Allen (Dmitri), Douglass
Dumbrille (Grilov), Gene Lockhart (Lushin),
Charles Waldron (The University President),
Thurston Hall (The Editor), Johnny Arthur (The
Clerk), Mrs. Patrick Campbell (The Pawnbroker),
Rafaelo Ottiano (Landlady), and Michael Mark
(Painter Prisoner).

CRIME AND PUNISHMENT exemplifies an era in which it
was considered uplifting to squeeze the five-foot shelf
into the thirty-five millimeter screen. Hollywood justi-
fied its cannibalization of the classics by arguing that
what the industry gained in prestige it repaid in
popularization as millions of moviegoers discovered for
the first time what fun there was in great literature.
Reviewers generally hailed this trend since it allowed
them to display their comparative lit insights in a show
biz setting.

CRIME AND PUNISHMENT (1935). Peter Lorre, Robert Allen,
Marian Marsh

There is little point, however, in discussing Dostoevsky in the context of Sternberg's career. CRIME
AND PUNISHMENT was a relatively impersonal assignment for the director. He inherited script, cast, and
miscast with his two-picture Columbia contract, and he
proceeded to demonstrate his efficiency and frugality as a
studio director. All through his life, Sternberg has had
to prove that he was sensible and intelligent and not at
all the impractical genius of his reputation, but his
penny-wise professionalism probably made him more
enemies in Hollywood than his pound-foolish personality. From a purely tactical standpoint, Sternberg might
better have played his creative eccentricity for all it was
worth than frighten the front offices and craft unions
with his composite expertise. There was simply no
place for a Renaissance spirit in the guild medievalism
of Hollywood in the thirties.

Yet even under the most ideal conditions imaginable,
Sternberg would have been singularly miscast as a
Dostoevskian director. For one thing, his dominant
gestures are more physical than metaphysical; for
another, he has no genuine grasp of evil and criminality
as facts of life and facets of character. Instead
Sternberg displays his own stylish bravado through the
Napoleonic and Nietzschean poses of Peter Lorre's
"Raskolnikov." The director then counters this mock
megalomania with Edward Arnold's "Inspector Porfiry,"
a father figure too civilized to mind youthful impetu-
osity and too mature not to care about its emotional
consequences. Sternberg claims to have had trouble
directing Arnold, and Lorre was generally considered
miscast, but the viewer who can ignore Dostoevsky's
lost nuances can see in the Arnold-Lorre relationship a
restatement of the duality of the male in Sternbergian
cinema, a duality most delicately expressed by Clive
Brook and George Bancroft in UNDERWORLD. Sternberg's males reflect not only the different aspects of his
personality, but also the different periods of his life.
As Sternberg gets older, a paternal and magisterial
attitude toward his own youth emerges through the
characterizations of Lionel Atwill in THE DEVIL IS A
WOMAN, Edward Arnold in CRIME AND PUNISHMENT,
and Walter Huston in THE SHANGHAI GESTURE.

Critics of the time preferred Pierre Chenal's version
of CRIME AND PUNISHMENT (France 1935) with Harry
Baur's "Porfiry" playing fat, smug cat to Pierre Blan-
char's lean, sensitively sniffing mouse. Baur and Blan-

char were undoubtedly showier than Arnold and Lorre, but Chenal's tantalizing theatrics hardly compared with the mood and feeling generated by the more reflective style of the Sternberg version. Tala Birell as a girl of the streets is not in a class with an Evelyn Brent or a Marlene Dietrich or a Sylvia Sidney, but Sternberg does what he can with the jaunty angle of a perky Michael Arlen hat, somewhat obscuring her lack of personality. Lorre's "Raskolnikov" treats her with all the gallantry befitting a damsel of destiny, and Sternberg even creates a distinctively un-Dostoevskian mood of shimmering nostalgia when Lorre gazes fatalistically into shining streaks of muddy water, and the girl muses alongside him with an almost equivalent despair. Curiously, the effect is moving apart from any particularly meaningful context, and Lorre, like Phillips Holmes in AN AMERICAN TRAGEDY, reveals an unexpected sweetness which is the hallmark of the Sternbergian hero.

1936 THE KING STEPS OUT (Columbia) Directed by Josef von Sternberg. Produced by William Perlberg. Script by Sidney Buchman from the operetta "Cissy" by Hubert and Ernst Marischka, based on the play "Cissy" by Ernst Decsey and Gustav Hohn. Photographed by Lucien Ballard. Sets by Stephen Goosens. Costumes by Ernst Dryden. Ballet by Albertina Rasch. Music by Fritz Kreisler arranged by Howard Jackson. Songs: "Stars in My Eyes," "Madly in Love," "Learn How to Lose," and "What Shall Remain?" by Fritz Kreisler (music) and Dorothy Fields (lyrics). With Grace Moore (Cissy), Franchot Tone (Franz Josef), Walter Connolly (Maximilian), Raymond Walburn (von Kempen), Victor Jory (Palfi), Elizabeth Risdon (Sofia), Nana Bryant (Louise), Frieda Inescourt (Helena), Thurston Hall (Major), Herman Bing (Pretzelberger), George Hassell (Herlicka), and John Arthur (Chief of Secret Police).

THE KING STEPS OUT hardly deserves any detailed analysis. The story, based on the life of Elizabeth of Austria, thrusts Grace Moore and Franchot Tone into the realm of happy Hapsburgs where the melodies of Fritz Kreisler guide true love past masquerades and misunderstandings. Franchot Tone's "Franz Josef" falls in love with Grace Moore's "Cissy," but she pretends to be a commoner, and he is betrothed to a princess, and "Cissy" is really the sister of his betrothed. Walter Connolly's "Maximilian," father of "Cissy," cajoles the royal sweethearts into marriage when he is not cadging steins of beer from Herman Bing's innkeeper and rolling guttural comedy r-r-r-relief. In his study of Sternberg, Curtis Harrington notes that the director painted the trees aluminum here as in THE SCARLET EMPRESS. This poetic tradition has been perpetuated by Max Ophuls with trees painted a glorious gold in LOLA MONTES, and by Michelangelo Antonioni with trees painted a petrified gray in THE RED DESERT. THE KING STEPS OUT is certainly Sternberg's whitest film in terms of visual texture, but he lacks Lubitsch's lightness and conviction with the operetta form. (It might be noted that a German production of "Cissy" in the late fifties made Romy Schneider a star.)

Grace Moore, like most screen sopranos, presents special problems to a director: first and foremost, a soprano on the wings of song must dominate her décor either with solitary close-ups or rapt two-shots with a frozen-smile admirer. In the case of close-ups, subsequent reaction shots of enchanted listeners complete the process of turning the cinema into a concert hall. Nevertheless, Sternberg managed to obtain moderately charming performances from Franchot Tone and Walter Connolly, and a certain semblance of comedy style is discernible when the heroine is not being excessively coy. Grace Moore's glacial personality was actually seen to greater advantage in Victor Schertzinger's ONE NIGHT OF LOVE (1934) where the warmth of Puccini heated up the sound track. In THE KING STEPS OUT, Fritz Kreisler's melodies tinkle a bit too icily to melt her remarkable reserve. Puccini aside, however, Grace Moore was in no sense a Sternbergian siren. Ultimately, the conventions of operetta were too frothy for the director's sensibility to take hold. Sternberg had hitherto had more dramatically compelling characters with which to fantasize his feelings, and consequently the Bavarian schmaltz of THE KING STEPS OUT fails even as an exercise in style.

1937 CLAUDIUS (Unfinished) Directed and written by Josef von Sternberg. Produced by Alexander Korda. From the novel *I, Claudius* by Robert Graves. Photographed by Georges Perinal. Sets by Vincent Korda. Choreography by Agnes De Mille. With Charles Laughton, Merle Oberon, Flora Robson, Robert Newton, and Emlyn Williams.

"God must have been very angry with me when I attempted to make CLAUDIUS," is Sternberg's summation of his difficulties with Charles Laughton in this ill-fated venture. A BBC documentary on the production confirms the clashes of temperament involved, but the two reels of footage shot for CLAUDIUS bears out Sternberg's prognosis: "That part of the film which was completed is on record as proof that in spite of his antics it might have been a memorable film." It might indeed. CLAUDIUS contained all the thematic and stylistic potentialities for a genuinely great film. Dirk Bogarde, who narrated the documentary, actually compares Laughton's coronation speech to the Roman Senate with Laurence Olivier's St. Crispin's Day speech in HENRY V, and the comparison is not inapt. The casting was impeccable with Laughton flanked by Flora Robson, Emlyn Williams, and Robert Newton. Merle Oberon's "Messalina" is slightly more conjectural, but, all things considered, she would have been more than adequate. The theme of virtue finding its own reward before yielding to the folly of megalomania is one very close to Sternberg, and the filmed scene of Laughton groveling before Emlyn Williams' hysterical Caligula is directed with a profound compassion for Claudius and an incisive insight into the paradox that man must sink completely into the mud of his limitations before he can rise to his aspirations.

When Merle Oberon was seriously injured in an automobile accident, the production was permanently shelved. All the participants agree, however, that Miss Oberon's accident was more a pretext than a cause for calling a halt. Merle Oberon aside, of course, the big loser was Sternberg. CLAUDIUS turned out to be his last, lost chance to recoup all his former reputation.

The BBC documentary records Emlyn Williams' violent hostility to Sternberg, and Flora Robson's bemused tolerance of this most colorful of Hollywood directors. More revealing than either is the script girl who recalls that the director cut every frame of CLAUDIUS in his mind. Sternberg emerges from the documentary as an undeniable force in the process of creation, and even his enemies confirm his artistic presence in every foot of film he ever shot.

Sternberg's misadventures did not end with CLAUDIUS. From 1937 to 1938, he prepared to film Zola's *Germinal,* only to be thwarted in his production plans by his own illness. He had also considered filming Pirandello's *Six Characters in Search of an Author* with Max Reinhardt playing the stage manager, but nothing had materialized. At last in October, 1938, he signed a one-picture contract with Metro to direct Hedy Lamarr in a story tentatively titled NEW YORK CINDERELLA but worked on it for only eighteen days. Frank Borzage finished the picture, but it was shelved until W. S. Van Dyke reshot some of the sequences. In 1940, it was released as I TAKE THIS WOMAN to a unanimously unfavorable press.

Sternberg had probably been signed for the film because of his reputation with Dietrich. Hedy Lamarr was no Dietrich, of course; her beauty was static rather than kinetic, the province more of photography than cinematography, and Metro's method of "humanizing" her exotic appeal probably did not appeal to Sternberg. He fulfilled his Metro contract with a Wallace Beery gangster vehicle entitled SERGEANT MADDEN under circumstances reminiscent of the events that had led up to UNDERWORLD. (Before signing with Metro, he had tidied up THE GREAT WALTZ for them.) Unfortunately lightning failed to strike twice, and SERGEANT MADDEN was no UNDERWORLD.

1939 SERGEANT MADDEN (Metro-Goldwyn-Mayer) Directed by Josef von Sternberg. Produced by J. Walter Ruben. Script by Wells Root based on the story "A Gun in His Hand" by William A. Ullman. Photographed by John Seitz. Sets by Cedric Gibbons and Randall Duell. Montage effects by Peter Ballbusch. Edited by Conrad A. Nervig. Music by Dr. William Axt. With Wallace Beery (Shaun Madden), Tom Brown (Al Boylan, Jr.), Alan Curtis (Dennis Madden), Laraine Day (Eileen Daly), Fay Holden (Mary Madden), Marc Lawrence ("Piggy" Ceders), Marian Martin (Charlotte), David Gorcey ("Punchy"), and Donald Haines, Ben Welden,

Etta McDaniel, John Kelly, Horace MacMahon, Neil Fitzgerald, and Dickie Jones.

SERGEANT MADDEN is of more sociological than aesthetic interest despite Sternberg's visually striking direction. The plot is obnoxiously conformist in the mode of the police propaganda of the time. Wallace Beery's sanctimonious "Sergeant Madden" has two sons, one natural and one adopted, and naturally it is the natural son who goes bad after being framed as a "killer cop" by Marc Lawrence's engagingly evil gangster. Beery finally goes after his bad son himself, but the prodigal atones for his misdeeds and the trouble he has caused his father, brother, wife, and baby son by letting himself be shot by the law. The moral, strikingly similar to that of Joe May's ASPHALT in the twenties, is that society transcends family. The notion of a blood son being morally inferior to an adopted one is another movie cliché, perhaps most strikingly executed in E. A. Dupont's A SON COMES HOME (1936).

SERGEANT MADDEN also partakes of some of the period's grubby pessimism about people who are too ambitious for their own good. Bad Son Alan Curtis is too quick with a gun to become a good, honest, plodding cop like "Sergeant Madden," while Good Son Tom Brown is suitably dull and mediocre for the modest demands of middle-class life. Laraine Day is lovely in this early stage of her career although she has little to do here except look longingly at Tom Brown and Alan Curtis, mostly from a bed in the maternity ward where moral issues are somewhat elemental.

Sternberg's distinctive framing and filters give the movie a UFA look, and at times one can almost see the ghost of Jannings in Beery's unusually restrained performance. Unfortunately, the characters are too unambiguous for Sternberg's subtlety to find expression. If the characterizations in THE KING STEPS OUT are a branch of puppetry, the characterizations in SERGEANT MADDEN are a bundle of priggishness.

1941 THE SHANGHAI GESTURE (United Artists) Directed by Josef von Sternberg. Produced by Arnold Pressburger. Script by Josef von Sternberg, Karl Vollmöller, Geza Herczeg, and Jules Furthman based on the play by John Colton. Photographed by Paul Ivano. Art direction by Boris Leven.

Sets by Howard Bristol. Murals by Key Luke. Edited by Sam Winston. Miss Munson's costumes by Royer. Miss Tierney's costumes by Oleg Cassini. Wigs by Hazel Rogers. Music by Richard Hageman. Associate Producer: Albert de Courville. With Gene Tierney (Poppy), Walter Huston (Sir Guy Charteris), Victor Mature (Dr. Omar), Ona Munson ("Mother" Gin Sling), Phyllis Brooks (Dixie Pomeroy), Albert Basserman (Commissioner), Maria Ouspenskaya (Amah), Eric Blore (Bookkeeper), Ivan Lebedeff (Gambler), Mike Mazurki (Coolie), Clyde Fillmore (Comprador), Rex Evans (Counselor Brooks), Grayce Hampton (Social Leader), Michael Delmatoff (Bartender), Marcel Dalio (Croupier), Mikhail Rasumni (Cashier), and John Abbott (Escort).

THE SHANGHAI GESTURE is a marvelous joke on the zeitgeist of the forties. At a time when screen censorship was so rigid that films of the early thirties like ARROWSMITH and A FAREWELL TO ARMS were reissued only after extensive scissoring for salacity, THE SHANGHAI GESTURE had no ostensible subject except the decadence and depravity of a horde of people who seem to have been left behind by history and the SHANGHAI EXPRESS. Of course, all the depravity could not be spelled out exactly. "Mother" Goddam's joy house becomes "Mother" Gin Sling's gambling casino, and it now is too late for anyone to say, "It took more than one man to change my name to Shanghai Lily." Nor is it possible for characters to inhale opium as in the bygone days of Richard Barthelmess' BROKEN BLOSSOMS and potent poppy seeds. Gene Tierney's name in THE SHANGHAI GESTURE is Poppy, but that is the only clue to her degradation the censors will permit. It is strange to remember that all narcotics were legal in America until 1924, and that this noblest of noble experiments intersects film history at a point where an allegedly Victorian director like Griffith can be more explicit about the subject than an allegedly Baudelairean director like Sternberg.

Sternberg was invited by Arnold Pressburger to bring John Colton's vintage stage shocker to the screen. Sternberg added the two crucial characters of Doctor Omar and Phyllis Brooks' Dixie Pomeroy to the denizens of his den of iniquity. Omar, "Doctor of

Nothing," is an inspired comic creation, a languid sybarite full of fearfully transparent banalities, more impressive to the worldly sophisticates at the card tables than to a Brooklyn chorus girl like Dixie Pomeroy. The wonderful thing about Omar is that he knows how ridiculous he is, and yet he knows he has enough style to impose his personality in a setting so devoid of will and purpose. As Sternberg guided Mature through his performance, the director reclining in a cot as part of his convalescence, was it possible that he recognized something of himself in Omar? Sternberg had always been kidded about his "von" and his alleged pants-pressing past in Brooklyn, and there was undoubtedly a conflict in his own personality between Austria and America, between pretense and pragmatism. The wonderful thing about Sternberg is that he can see the humor in the conflict and render it artistically.

There is some of this humorous clash of pretense and pragmatism in MOROCCO between Dietrich and Cooper, but a wonderfully warm reconciliation between the two as well. At this point in his career, the contrast of two worlds is rich with lyrical promise for Sternberg as Dietrich and Cooper flow together from opposite ends of Sternberg's universe. By the time of THE SCARLET EMPRESS, the American presence is somewhat harsher in the person of Louise Dresser, the fishwife empress who always knows what she wants and how to get it. Sternberg himself is represented by the Europeanized Americans like Menjou in MOROCCO, and Atwill in THE DEVIL IS A WOMAN, and the tone becomes increasingly bitter as the years go on, but by the time of THE SHANGHAI GESTURE Sternberg is far enough away from the conflict to see the humor of his own masquerade, and Omar is his comic testament, his fey Falstaff, as the voice in ANATAHAN is his unseen Lear.

Phyllis Brooks, one of those miraculously minor figures who define an era better than its major figures, is an obvious counterpoint to the exotically beautiful Gene Tierney, a buck-toothed all-American Broadway beauty who made George Jean Nathan and Richard

The banquet table as Sternberg's battlefield. THE SHANGHAI GESTURE (1942). At one end of the table the older generation, Ona Munson, Maria Ouspenskaya, Walter Huston, is arrayed in opposition to Victor Mature, Phyllis Brooks, and Gene Tierney (unseen) at the other end

Watts lose their heads, but who was transformed by Sternberg into a vaguely Eurasian standard of sophistication for the forties. This is the first time that Sternberg's camera has witnessed the complete disintegration of a female mystique, and he may have added the comedy presences of Omar and Dixie as a means of cushioning the shock. What happens to a woman when she loses her style and mystery is not a pleasant thing to watch, especially for Sternberg. What Tierney's Poppy lacks here so crucially is not so much character as humor, intelligence and an appreciation of the absurd. Passion makes her oblivious to parody, and she fails to notice Omar's ridiculously furtive gesture in concealing their kiss. To emphasize the ridiculousness, Sternberg shoots Mature's gesture from the far side so that Mature is framing rather than concealing the kiss as far as the movie audience is concerned. This apparently gratuitous gesture might be compared with Cooper's use of the fan to conceal his kissing Dietrich from the movie audience, a gesture Sternberg photographed from the near side so as to indicate that there was something genuine to conceal in the Dietrich-Cooper relationship. It follows with poetic logic that the ridiculousness of the Tierney-Mature relationship is revealed rather than concealed.

The rest of the plot is entrusted to Walter Huston and Ona Munson as old lovers confronting each other as total strangers, their enmity rising out of the ashes of an ancient love which we must take less on faith than fantasy. Yet real pastness is meaningless in a languorously stylised world in which all sense of time is negated by the metaphorical circle of the roulette wheel cybernetically descended from the dredge of THE SALVATION HUNTERS, the assembly line of AN AMERICAN TRAGEDY, and the banquet tables of THE SCARLET EMPRESS.

Nevertheless, the civilized graces persist even in the midst of all this futility, and characters continue to consider their fate with the utmost seriousness. Ivan Lebedeff's gambler apologizes to Mother Gin Sling for attempting suicide at the gaming table and then touchingly kisses her hand for extending him more credit. Mike Mazurki's oversized coolie becomes an understated metteur-en-scène and figure of fate. "You likee Chinee New Year?" Huston asks Mazurki with condescending mockery. Much later, Mazurki hurls the question back at Huston with what can be described as poetic justice. Huston thinks he has heard the shot that means his degraded daughter is now dead, but he cannot be sure because of the noise of firecrackers in Sternberg's Shanghai street, no wider than the width of the screen. Mazurki's "You likee Chinee New Year?" thus becomes the last lyrical line of a dramatic poem.

Madame Gin Sling prepares for her last dinner by constructing wax replicas of her guests. By arranging these replicas at the table, she creates the illusion of manipulating the destinies of the beings these replicas represent. Similarly, Sternberg's characters are generally only replicas of real people, but these replicas are endowed with real feelings, usually Sternberg's. Some of the minor replicas like John Abbott's simpering escort for Gene Tierney may be over-caricatured. William Powell's revolutionary turned director in THE LAST COMMAND and Ullrich Haupt's doomed cuckold in MOROCCO may be psychologically obscure. Yet, for the most part, Sternberg's characters derive their emotional resonance not from the specifications of the scenario, but from a curious intensity of expression in the style of Sternberg's direction.

Certainly the vibrant feelings of THE SHANGHAI GESTURE cannot be attributed to John Colton's stage shocker, nor even to Jules Furthman's flair for expressively epigrammatic dialogue. The weary grown-ups —Walter Huston, Ona Munson, Albert Basserman, Maria Ouspenskaya—look past their mature adolescence—Victor Mature and Phyllis Brooks—to their spoiled childhood incarnated in Gene Tierney, who makes her dramatic entrance at the last of Mother Gin Sling's dinners through the kind of meaningful memory filter that the remade Kim Novak enters for Stewart's inspection in VERTIGO. Huston looks at his disheveled daughter as Sternberg himself might look at his own disordered life. From THE SALVATION HUNTERS to ANATAHAN, Sternberg's recurring theme is self-awakening, and we have been fortunate in having had directors like Sternberg and Renoir and Dreyer and Ford and Chaplin and Welles who could show us so expressively on film how an artist can record his entire life on a moving strip of celluloid.

What is most felicitous in THE SHANGHAI GESTURE and least appreciated in Sternberg's films generally is the sheer beauty and meaningful grace of physical gestures and movements—the way his players walk, the way they grasp objects and fondle fabrics, the way they light cigarettes and flare the smoke through their nostrils, and the way they eat and drink. In the realm of physical expressiveness, Sternberg is supreme.

Needless to say, this world of gesture and movement is not lacking in Freudian overtones, and recent analyses by such neo-Freudian critics as Lo Duca, Raymond Durgnat, and O. O. Green have helped clear away some cobwebs from the traditional critiques of Sternberg. Unfortunately, such analyses seem to operate as validly with the unconscious and the accidental as with the conscious and the intentional. If THE SHANGHAI GESTURE abounds with symbols and gestures of impotence, castration, onanism and transvestism, so do KING KONG, TARZAN THE APE MAN, FRANKENSTEIN, and FREAKS. Yet these latter films can hardly be said to represent the conscious art of THE SHANGHAI GESTURE, where all the gestures and movements of human bodies express the rapture of an artist's soul.

1943 THE TOWN (United States Office of War Information) Directed by Josef von Sternberg. Produced by Phillip Dunne. Written by Joseph Krumgold. Photographed by Larry Madison on location in Madison, Indiana.

Sternberg tells the story of the time he came back from shooting some footage for THE TOWN on a suitably sunny day and being told by his superiors that documentaries were shot only on rainy days. This kind of anecdote is not calculated to endear him to those who believe that the high point of American cinema was THE PLOW THAT BROKE THE PLAINS, but Sternberg has never been highly regarded by realists anyway. THE TOWN itself is nevertheless very gracefully photographed and very skillfully edited as it describes a small American town in 1943. The narration is unctuously affirmative as it eulogizes Madison, Indiana, as a veritable melting pot of many European civilizations, but the images counter the flow of verbal banality with vivid details of daily life. There is not an ugly frame or an awkward cut or an unnecessary movement in the entire film. From the confidential intimacy of an elderly couple in a restaurant to the pleasingly scenic shot of a steamboat on the Ohio River, Sternberg's sense of composition and continuity is beautiful to behold. THE TOWN is ultimately the director's most sustained exposure to reality, and all that proves is that

what the documentary film lost, the dream film gained. THE TOWN is not particularly valuable aesthetically despite Sternberg's expert craftsmanship. It is instead a historical document of a time and place in human history, but the crudest newsreel footage is equally valuable in the context of pastness. The clothes people wore, the cars they drove, the streets they walked, the shops they patronized, the homes they inhabited, the work they did, and the amusements they enjoyed: these are the poignantly nostalgic details of a documentary like THE TOWN. Yet the nostalgia would be no less poignant if the direction were much cruder. Sternberg the artist is consequently superfluous in the realm of the fact film. Yet THE TOWN survives as Sternberg's testament to the proposition that after UNDERWORLD, MOROCCO, and SHANGHAI EXPRESS there is nothing to directing a documentary.

In 1946 Sternberg served as color consultant for David O. Selznick on DUEL IN THE SUN, directing one week's shooting of the picture while King Vidor was ill, but otherwise serving in an increasingly vague capacity. In recent years Vidor has confirmed Sternberg's limited contribution to the film and expressed regret that Sternberg's talents had not been more frequently utilized in Hollywood since that time.

Rounding out Sternberg's unrealized projects is a script called *The Seven Bad Years* concerning what the director describes as "man's fixation on an infantile level." Sternberg's description of the subject in his autobiography (pp. 279–80) makes it sound excessively didactic for a fictional film, and it is difficult to determine, therefore, what sort of movie he had in mind.

1951 JET PILOT (Howard Hughes Productions-Universal) Directed by Josef von Sternberg. Produced and written by Jules Furthman. Photographed by Winton C. Hoch. Aerial photography by Philip C. Cochran. Art direction by Albert S. D'Agostino and Feild Gray. Set decoration by Darrell Silvera and Harley Miller. Music by Bronislau Kaper. Musical direction by C. Bakaleinikoff. Editorial supervision by James Wilkinson. Edited by Michael R. McAdam, Harry Marker, and William M. Moore. Costumes by Michael Woulfel. With John Wayne (Colonel Shannon), Janet Leigh (Anna), Jay C. Flippen

(Major General Black), Paul Fix (Major Rexford), Richard Rober (George Rivers), Roland Winters (Colonel Sokolov), Hans Conried (Colonel Matoff), Ivan Triesault (General Langrad), John Bishop (Major Sinclair), Perdita Chandler (Georgia Rexford), Joyce Compton (Mrs. Simpson), Denver Pyle (Mr. Simpson), and members of the U. S. Air Force.

As a unique demonstration of right-wing camp on a comic strip level, JET PILOT may be ahead of its time through all eternity. Begun in 1951 and finally released in 1957, it anticipated many of the conceits of DR. STRANGELOVE and the James Bond series, but as Jean-Luc Godard has observed, the zany comedy of the conception clashed with the dramatic pictorialism of Sternberg's execution, and audiences failed to realize that they were watching a hilarious comedy. Whatever proportion of credit or censure is due to Howard Hughes, Jules Furthman, or Sternberg, the film is much more enduringly enjoyable than its reputation would indicate. JET PILOT reduces the Cold War to an animated cartoon where planes enjoy a more active sex life than human beings, and it does so with marvelously high spirits and uninhibited plot invention. The idea of Janet Leigh being a Russian jet pilot sent to entice John Wayne to defect to the Reds might startle even Terry Southern with its audacity. Jules Furthman, veteran scenarist for both Sternberg and Hawks, is made of sterner stuff. Wayne pretends to succumb to Leigh's wiles, and finds himself in a right-wing cartoonist's version of the Soviet Slave State complete with sneering commissars and brainwashing opiates. Finally, however, Karl Marx runs a poor second to a thick, juicy American steak, and Leigh and Wayne escape back to the U. S. A.

The much-admired pre-credit sequence of DR. STRANGELOVE which smirks at the spectacle of a jet bomber being refueled in mid-air is mild next to the lusty equivalent in JET PILOT. The aerial sequences are particularly exhilarating because there is no attempt at naturalistic cockpit sound and dialogue. The soundtrack is unvarying even in aerial long-shot so that Wayne and Leigh are not so much *in* their planes as interchangeable with them. After a while, the aerial animism by which planes equal people becomes comi-

cally lyrical, and the film soars in an ecstatic flight of speed, grace, and color.

On reflection, however, the humor and sensuality in JET PILOT seem somewhat too boisterous for Sternberg's established taste, and neither John Wayne nor Janet Leigh strikes the right casting note. Wayne, like Victor McLaglen in DISHONORED, is more at home in the John Ford galaxy, and Janet Leigh belongs to the Hitchcockian universe of PSYCHO and the Wellesian world of TOUCH OF EVIL. In JET PILOT, Wayne and Leigh remain raw material in terms of any discernibly Sternbergian style, but the picture is still highly entertaining if apparently meaningless.

1952 MACAO (RKO Radio Pictures) Directed by Josef von Sternberg (and, in the last stages of production, Nicholas Ray). Produced by Alex Gottlieb. Script by Bernard C. Schoenfeld, and Stanley Rubin based on a story by Bob Williams. Photographed by Harry J. Wild. Art direction by Albert S. D'Agostino and Ralph Berger. Set decoration by Darrell Silvera and Harley Miller. Costumes by Michael Woulfe. Edited by Samuel E. Beetley and Robert Golden. Musical direction by C. Bakaleinikoff. Songs: "One for My Baby" by Johnny Mercer and Harold Arlen; "Ocean Breeze" and "You Kill Me" by Jule Styne and Leo Robin. With Robert Mitchum (Nick Cochran), Jane Russell (Julie Benson), William Bendix (Lawrence Trumble), Thomas Gomez (Lieutenant Sebastian), Gloria Grahame (Margie), Brad Dexter (Halloran), Edward Ashley (Martin Stewart), Philip Ahn (Itzumi), Vladimir Sokolov (Kwan Sum Tang), and Don Zelaya (Gimpy).

Sternberg's contribution to MACAO is exclusively stylistic, and there is no evidence, internal or external, of any deeper involvement than that. The objective core of the plot is mouldy even by the sordid standards of the genre, and it would be difficult to argue that Sternberg's few visual coups constitute a triumph of form over content. The essential unity of form and content in most of Sternberg's films, all perhaps except for THE KING STEPS OUT, SERGEANT MADDEN, and MACAO, indicates how superficial mere style can be. Curiously, there is a tinny echo of MOROCCO in the opening sequence in which Robert Mitchum and William Bendix compete for Jane Russell's attentions on a steamer disembarking at Macao. Yet, though the situation is the same, the issues are entirely different, and the characters are soon enmeshed in a wearisome intrigue involving jewel smuggling, corruption, murder, and the necessity of luring the villain past the three-mile limit of Macao's territorial waters. Thomas Gomez' venal police official is the only interesting characterization, although Vladimir Sokolov's blind coolie is pointedly picturesque. Jane Russell adds a new dimension to the sullenness Sternberg first detected in Georgia Hale in THE SALVATION HUNTERS, and Gloria Grahame is equally unsympathetic in a part that drifts into pointlessness. Sternberg reportedly had a difficult time directing these two ladies whose intransigence during the shooting of MACAO has become a minor legend.

Sternberg's stylistic contributions include a feathery flurry from the pillow Mitchum thrusts into the whirring fan with which Russell assaults him, a view through waterfront netting of Bendix being stabbed to death, the kinetic effect of a chase across floats bobbing up and down with each step, and the various stylistic subterfuges employed to conceal the meaninglessness of the action with the menace of the atmosphere. Nicholas Ray's direction is uncredited, but his participation in the last stages of production has been confirmed by both Sternberg and Producer Alex Gottlieb. It seems that Ray shot the climactic fist fight between Mitchum and the villainous Brad Dexter, and this sort of thing was never Sternberg's cup of tea.

1953 ANATAHAN   (Daiwa Productions-Towa/Pathe-Contemporary) Directed, produced, written, narrated, and photographed by Josef von Sternberg. From a true story by Michiro Maruyama. Japanese dialogue by Asano. Sets by Kono. Music by Akira Ifukube. With Akemi Negishi (Queen Bee), Tadashi Suganuma (Husband), Kisaburo Sawamura, Shoji Nakayama, Jun Fujikawa, Hiroshi Kondo, Shozo Miyashita (the five Drones), Tsuruemon Bando and Kikuji Onoe (the two Skippers), Kokuriro Kinoya (the Musician), Dajiro Tamura, Tadashi Kitagawa, and Takashi Suzuki (the Homesick Men), and Shiro Amikura (the Patriot)

If it should indeed turn out that ANATAHAN is the last film to be directed by Josef von Sternberg, it would mark a fittingly personal conclusion to the film-maker's career. Sternberg himself regards ANATAHAN as his best film, a judgment both his defenders and his detractors would probably reject. But then ANATAHAN is a very private film, probably Sternberg's most private, and its ironic humor is inaccessible to most audiences. By conventional standards, the plot is virtually pointless, and the characters obvious to the point of obscurity. Sternberg's commentary, at times contrapuntal and at times apparently superfluous to the narrative, would appeal only to specialists in his career. The rest of the audience will always be outraged by the spectacle of a director journeying to Kyoto to fabricate a hermetically sealed studio film allegedly describing an adventure on a Pacific Island during and after World War II. When Sternberg was asked by a French critic why he had gone to the Far East to enclose himself within a studio set he could have constructed on a Hollywood back lot, Sternberg replied simply and magnificently: "Because I am a poet."

Far from apologizing for the studied artificiality of his mise-en-scène, Sternberg confounds his realistically oriented critics by claiming that he erred only on the side of reality in allowing footage of authentically foamy ocean waves to intrude on the dream-like décor of his ANATAHAN, an enchanted Eden which he willed into existence purely to project his own fantasies of life, memory, desire, and death. To this imaginary island called Anatahan come twelve survivors from a symbolic shipwreck on a painted sea (Hollywood?). They are all identified as members of the Japanese Imperial Navy, and they seem both impassive and indistinguishable to the Western eye.

Sternberg, like most directors, is a creature of necessity, and must take his chances where he can find them, but it would seem almost logical that the director of SHANGHAI EXPRESS and THE SHANGHAI GESTURE would eventually be drawn to an Orient *jamais vu* he had always made seem *déjà vu*. Also, Sternberg's insistence on controlling every last expression and intonation of his actors until at times it seemed, particularly to the players concerned, that he was reducing the human face to mask-like inscrutability, and the human voice to a monotone of recited ritual, must always have attracted him to the Orient where facial impassivity is actually a means of "saving face."

Normally it is considered unwise for a director to suppress the natural personality of his performers, at least to the degree that Sternberg attempted. The whole point of his direction of actors, however, is remarkably consistent with his theory of art. All his characters, Sternberg insists, are projections of himself, and, as such, are mere details of his décor, or, at most, ghostly figures in his projected dreams. Nothing really happens in ANATAHAN; every incident is filtered through a thick veil of remembrance and regret. A man is shot, but we neither see nor hear the bullet, and there is no real blood, only drums and pantomime to emphasize that the shooting occurred long ago in a silent dream with an off-screen commentary. Throughout his career Sternberg has tended to muffle his violence, and even in such early gangster classics as UNDERWORLD and THUNDERBOLT, the gunplay is invested with the dream-like deliberateness of ritual and ceremony.

Obviously, the same man wrote the commentary for ANATAHAN, the titles for THE SALVATION HUNTERS, and the prose for *Fun in a Chinese Laundry,* and the same literary lapses occur over a forty-year period. Sternberg's addiction to overly abstract rhetoric and overly elegant turns of phrase is a fault he shares most conspicuously with Chaplin. Less obviously, both men share a similarly ironic temperament which enables them to cast a cold eye at their own conceits.

Unfortunately, this ultra-Pirandellian penchant is much harder to detect in direction than in acting, and Sternberg's disadvantage in not being an actor-director like Chaplin, Stroheim, and Welles was that his ironies remained invisible to the general public. Consequently, the subtle humor of the Sternberg oeuvre as a whole has been overlooked by critics intent on confusing seriousness with solemnity.

What ultimately interests Sternberg in ANATAHAN is the spectacle of man's dignity and honor crumbling before the assault of desire. When the girl on the island is first introduced to the survivors, Sternberg's camera remains focused deliriously on the girl's beauty. This emphasis might be compared with a similar situation in Renoir's LA GRANDE ILLUSION where the Allied prisoners pause to stare at the impersonation of a chorus girl by a British soldier. Renoir's approach is humanist in the sense that he asks his audience to respond to the fraternal feeling of sexual longing shared by the prisoners. Sternberg, by contrast, asks the audience to respond to the spectacle of the woman herself, to the dark, mysterious beauty which obliterates reason, honor, dignity. Renoir wants us to love our fellow men. Sternberg wants us to understand the origin of man's folly. To understand but not to overcome. For Sternberg, Woman, in Truffaut's phrase, will always be supreme.

NOTES ON REFERENCES

The books and articles most frequently consulted for this study are as follows:

Cecelia Ager: "Optics on Roller Bearings," *Variety,* May 8, 1935.

Peter Bogdanovich: "Josef von Sternberg," *Movie,* Number 13, Summer 1965.

Patrick Brion: "Filmographie de Josef von Sternberg," *Cahiers du Cinéma,* Number 168, July 1965.

John Grierson: "Directors of the Thirties" from *Grierson on Documentary,* Harcourt, Brace, New York, 1947, edited by Forsyth Hardy, reprinted in *Film,* Simon & Schuster, 1959, edited by Daniel Talbot.

Curtis Harrington: *An Index to the Films of Josef von Sternberg,* Special Supplement to *Sight & Sound,* February 1949.

Aeneas Mackenzie: "Leonardo of the Lenses," *Life and Letters Today,* London 1936.

Susan Sontag: "Notes on 'Camp'," *Partisan Review,* Fall 1964, Volume XXXI, Number 4, pp. 515–530.

Josef von Sternberg: *Fun in a Chinese Laundry,* Macmillan, New York 1965.

Herman G. Weinberg: "Filmography" from *Josef von Sternberg, Editions Seghers,* Paris 1966.

Where there were discrepancies in the credits, we tended to be permissive and inclusive unless there was objective evidence to the contrary. Writing credits, in particular, will always be a bone of contention, but there is now little doubt that Sternberg participated, with or without credit, in the writing of his most meaningful films. Certainly, no mere literary figure could have written Sternberg's camera angles and compositions, which are as much a province of screenwriting as dialogue.

ANATAHAN (1954). Tadashi Suganuma and Okemi Negishi.
Courtesy Herman Weinberg

Josef von Sternberg
Back cover: Make-up and costume test
for Marlene Dietrich
in THE DEVIL IS A WOMAN (1935)